Sierra Songs & Descants:

Poetry & Prose of the Sierra

Sierra Songs & Descants:
Poetry & Prose of the Sierra

Edited by
Gail Rudd Entrekin
&
Kathryn Napier Stull

Managing Editor: Charles Entrekin
Nevada City, CA
2002

Hip Pocket Press
228 Commercial Street, # 138
Nevada City, CA 95959

Typesetting by Wordsworth
            San Geronimo, CA

Printing and distribution by Lightning Source, Inc.

Cover design by   Brook Design Group
            Nevada City, CA

Cover painting "The River" by Ingeborg Kroeninger

Photo of cover painting by Gene Crowe

Sincere thanks to Karla Arens, and most especially to Judy Crowe and
Liz Kellar for their many hours of proofreading help.

Order at www.hippocketpress.com

ISBN 0-917658-32-9

Permission of authors to reprint the following material is gratefully acknowledged.

Dan Bellm, "Aspens" and "Siren Song," from *Buried Treasure* (Cleveland State University Poetry Center, 1999).

Doc Dachtler, "Firewood," from *Tundra* (1999).

Ross Drago, "Across the Street" and "Waiting for the Bank to Open," chapters 19 and 28, respectively, from *Buffalo Boy* (Backbone Books, 1999).

Gail Rudd Entrekin, "Deep World" (*Birmingham Review*, 2002).

Molly Fisk, "At Home on the Page" (TWA's *Ambassador* magazine, 1998).

Oakley Hall, "Ambrose Bierce and the One-Eyed Jacks," Chapter 2 from the novel-in-progress of the same name (Viking, forthcoming).

James D. Houston, "Prologue from the Trail Notes of Patty Reed," from *Snow Mountain Passage* (Alfred A. Knopf, 2001).

Jeanne Wakatsuki Houston, "A Taste of Snow," from *Beyond Manzanar and Other Views of Asian American Womanhood* (Capra Press, 1985).

Belden Johnson, "Encounter Group," from *Snake Blossoms* (Berkeley Poets Workshop & Press, 1976).

Alicia Suskin Ostriker, "First Betrayal," from *Once More Out of Darkness & Other Poems* (Berkeley Poets Workshop & Press, 1974).

Utah Phillips, "The Old Guy Meets His Childhood Sweetheart," from *The Old Guy Poems* (Brownell Library Press, 1988).

Carlos Reyes, "Piute," from *A Suitcase Full of Crows* (Bluestem Press, 1995).

Marilee Richards, "Surviving" and "How an Older Man Makes Love," from *A Common Ancestor* (Hip Pocket Press, 1998).

Claudette Mork Sigg, "Mourning on Sandy Bar," from *Voices and Images of the Gold Rush* (Oakland Museum Writers on Site Project, 1998).

Steve Wilson, "Meditation on Birds Near Nightfall," from the *Christian Science Monitor* (2000).

All profits from *Sierra Songs & Descants* benefit
Literature Alive!

Table of Contents

Summer

Fall

Winter

Publisher's Preface

This anthology reflects, we believe, a style of writing that deserves recognition and celebration; it is a style peculiar to an aesthetic one finds most often in the Sierra Nevada and in the Northwestern United States in general. It is a style that is place-based, character-based, and story-based. It eschews the emptiness of abstractions, the social pressure of political correctness, and the simpering, wayward sentimentalities of postmodern authorial intrusions. This style of writing believes that beneath every human phenomenon lies concealed a discrepant reality, and that an advantage can be gained by bringing it to light, by "going under the surface" and bringing that discrepant piece of the puzzle up into consciousness. This kind of writing bears up under scrutiny; it reveals what is necessary for us all to know; it returns benefit for effort; it is a joy to behold; and it reminds us, finally, what is most gratifying to know — that we are a part of a larger reality, that we are not alone.

Charles Entrekin
Managing Editor
Hip Pocket Press

Foreword

by Sands Hall

Sierra. Spanish for "mountain."

For thousands of years these mountains were home to Native American tribes: the Maidu, the Navaho, the Washoe, among others. For a few centuries the area was claimed by Spain; then, for a few decades Mexico governed the area, after it wrested independence from its mother country. Until 1849 the only white men to make their way across the expanse of mountains were the occasional trapper and the even more occasional settler.

The Sierra Nevada, the white man found it was called. The snowy mountains. Then gold was discovered, changing forever the face, the inhabitants, and the language of these mountains.

When I was newly settled in Nevada County, a man invited me to join him for tea. Over our English Breakfast and chamomile, he asked if I knew why so many artists, as well as healers (therapists, bodyworkers, herbalists, and the like) are attracted to this area.

I hadn't really thought about it.

"Because of the gold that runs beneath the Sierra Nevada," he told me over his steaming cup. "Gold attracts those searching for wealth, of course. But have you ever stopped to consider why gold is such a magnet?"

I shook my head.

He leaned towards me. "It's an element with magical properties. It attracts artists and seekers, always has. Its monetary pull is merely one aspect of its mystical qualities."

At the time I found this amusing, even quaint. But living here and witnessing the number of artists, and, yes, healers (and artists are often healers, and vice versa) who live and work and, miraculously, succeed in the small communities of the Sierra Nevada, this conversation returns to me. And I think, why not?

The artists that congregate above the gold in the Sierra, specifi-cally in Nevada County, include musicians creating every conceivable type of music, painters, sculptors, photographers, filmmakers, actors, directors, designers — there are at least five theatre companies — and an extraordinary number of writers. Writers of fiction, poetry, essay, personal narrative, memoir, libretto; there are songwriters and screenwriters and playwrights, all mining, and shaping, words.

In 1995 Casey Walker, editor of *The Wild Duck Review*, and Joanna Robinson, at the time owner of the Nevada City bookstore, Harmony Books, decided to do something about all this literary gold. They founded an organization called Literature Alive!, whose original purpose was to give the wide range of literary voices in our community a time and place to be heard.

A board was created, nonprofit status established, its mission expanded: "To bring the living voice of literature to Nevada County."

Thus the prongs of Literature Alive's endeavors were put into place:

Individual Readings and Workshops: A writer, often brought from out of town, shares his or her writing, sometimes conducting a workshop the following day.

Listening to the Wild: An annual event held the same weekend as Earth Day, in which local writers, both published and fledgling, read from their works. The writing often explores aspects of nature or offers a perspective on "wild."

Wordslingers: Writers local and far-flung gather on a fall evening to share their perspectives, sometimes with a theme.

A year or two into Literature Alive's existence, the involvement and financial support of Charles and Gail Entrekin strengthened the organization's ability to pursue its goals. The Entrekins, both of whom are writers and teachers of writing, are the editors and publishers of Hip Pocket Press. They became publishers because they wanted to have a say in what counts as literature today. "The so-called `Academy' has such dominance," Charles Entrekin says. "Too often what is considered to be literature is influenced by political correctness or connection politics."

"Writers often don't have any kind of support system," Gail adds. "They're housewives or they work nine to five and in whatever free time they have they write, and then they scour the classified ads in *Poets and Writers Magazine*, or whatever, sending their poems or stories out, again and again and again. We wanted to provide a venue for some of the best of those voices to be heard."

"We also realized there was almost a Northern California/Nevada County literary style," Charles told me, "in the same way certain California landscape painters have a 'look,' a style that's recognizable. We're interested in drawing attention to it: A language of place. It seems important to honor that."

And so: *Sierra Songs & Descants.*

The pieces in this volume do not necessarily mention the Sierra nor does every writer represented live in or even near the mountains. The selections range widely and include fiction and poetry, essay and memoir, the humorous and the serious. For instance, novelist Oakley Hall provides an excerpt from the most recent release in his popular series of mysteries, *Ambrose Bierce and the One-Eyed Jacks.* Sandra Rockman gives us "True Confessions of a Reluctant Naturalist." Jeff Kane's insightful humor is represented by two of his *Karma Sierra* pieces, "Chock Full of Fiber" and "Guns Don't Kill People."

Among the poets sharing their gold is Doc Dachtler with "Tick Removal Cocktail" and his haunting "Firewood." George Keithley's luminous contributions include "What Is the Wild Love That Leads Us?" Donna Hanelin's "Dry Ranges" is included, as are haiku by Steve Sanfield. Molly Fisk's poems are included, as well as her essay, "At Home on the Page." Demian Entrekin provides "The Bright Night," a villanelle, that demanding poetic form in which lines of the poem must be used several times in a very precise prescription.

In the mid-1800s, Sam Foss wrote the famous quatrain that begins, "Bring me men to match my mountains." He gave himself the persona, the voice, as he saw it, of this marvelous new state, California.

> Bring me men to match my plains,
> Men with empires in their purpose,
> And new eras in their brains.

The poem doesn't scan very well, and the final line is quite awkward, but it stands as one of the many efforts made by artists who traversed — and traverse still — this territory, trying to capture its magnificence.

Mr. Foss' lines are in praise of men who would not only match but conquer the magnificent Sierra Nevada; that was the relationship, at the time, between men and wilderness. But the men and women who came to California to toil for gold, to provide services for those toiling for gold, and simply to settle, were often a literate bunch. They kept journals, they wrote letters home, they brought with them ideas about law, religion, slavery, suffrage — politics in all its forms — and, of course, finance. They were engineers, geologists, teachers,and clergymen, some of them fresh from the most prestigious schools in the East.

Also drawn to California were the Chinese, whose work built the transcontinental railway and whose culture and religion seeped into and altered that of the West. The Welsh, Irish, and Cornish brought their knowledge of hard-rock mining to the area, along with turns of phrase and a legendary ability with a joke. The language and cultural contributions of the Spanish and early Mexican citizens run as deep as veins of ore. And the natives, the earliest inhabitants of this area, left traces of language and art and craft that are only now beginning to be acknowledged and celebrated.

These and many other cultures contributed to the language of California, and of the Sierra. Place names give us a good sense of this heritage. We still call Tahoe, Coloma (originally Culoomah), and the Yuba and Truckee rivers by their native names. The territory's Hispanic background donated — in addition to Sierra Nevada — names like San Juan Ridge and Sacramento. Miners and mine owners made sure beloved Eastern states were represented: the Idaho Maryland — now the name of a main thoroughfare — and the Pennsylvania. Colfax, named eventually after Grant's vice-president, was originally called Illinoistown, which may explain nearby Chicago Park. Other names represent the steely-eyed humor of early residents:: the You Bet Mine (and Sure Bet Road), Greenhorn Creek, the towns of Humbug and Rough and Ready. Words with religious overtones were pilfered from the *Bible* and *The Book of Mormon*: Zion, Gethsemane, Piety Hill, Tribulation Trail, displaying the wit, zeal, and imagination of early settlers, qualities which continue to be exemplified by the writers who live in and depict the area today.

When Mr. Foss, in the voice of the Sierra, asked for those who could "match my mountains," those with "new eras in their brains," he may not have intended writers and artists to answer his call. Yet my friend who invited me to tea might well be right: there is something running in the lodes beneath this place, some mystery that pulled, and continues to pull, those who strive to capture, savor, and share the wonder of the Sierra. One result is a language of place, literature of this place.

Sierra Songs & Descants celebrates that literature.

What Is the Wild Love That Leads Us?

What is the wild love that leads us down
to the end of the flat canyon floor,
cluttered with leaves and branches blown
to earth and rotting in the rain,

urging us onto this trail,
tracking for mile after mile?
The rain holds behind us until
we stumble to find our footing where

we've waded into the iron cold snow
that all but covers a mountain meadow.
What is the wild love that leads us far
away from the long land below,

the hunt forgotten in the autumn air
full of flakes? By dark the storm
has died down and we see moonlight bloom
across the ridge. When we climb

beyond the prints of the small brown bear
and the last clean tracks of the deer
and fall into a circle by the fire,
what is the wild love that leads us here?

George Keithley

Spring

Sierra Songs & Descants

Susan Goldsmith Wooldridge

First Words

The words came without their numbers.

For awhile it was two by two
like animals onto the ark.

    Tangerine came with hustle
    splendor with taboo.

Some of the first words came with a little
electrical *ping* when they touched the ground.

They hadn't been uttered yet
and were all still shiny and intact.
Nothing had been broken by them yet.

Their colors, some stark, like the yellows,
were so bright no one (had anyone been present)
could look at them directly.
As if they'd just come from the sun.

"I would be ignorant as the dawn," Yeats said.
Words like this kept falling from somewhere.

Not like rain, though it was raining.
    Simulacrum
    redundant retank
all these words came and wouldn't stop coming,
    imbue, terrestrial, seed, soon,

in a rush
in wildest light
that first
wet morning.

Jacquie Bellon

Spring

Watch the daffodils
vacillating under
the rain
turn into umbrellas
petals shielding
pollen, nectar.
And so I
bend my head to shield my heart
hold still center
tremble at the edge
shed drops
kneel closer to
the earth
wait for the storm
to pass.

After four days of rain
the grapes have grown
another foot
grass reversing itself
young stems bent to the ground.
Only the irises stand tall
like ruined debutantes
after the ball.

Benjamin Jahn

It All Ends Up in the Same Place

I'll tell you about Spar McHugh, who Harve and me encountered on his last day among us, as they say. It was one week after Spar's store got shut down for sellin jug wine to some Indian kids who that same night burnt the schoolhouse to its foundation. After that, Spar's back door turned into an entrance, and he hawked his leftover stock at cut rates.

On this day the store was real dim — the windows boarded against sight from the highway that coursed through town. Gray light punched through nail holes in the plywood, leaked in around the sills. We milled around, stared at labels, tried to make them out. Spar cleared his pipe. "Don't you boys know what you're after?" He shoved his stump into his jeans pocket.

Harve picked out a cheap mash. "Cold beer," he said. "You got any a that?"

Spar spat on the floor. Behind him on a hook board hung bottle openers, corkscrews, and cig lighters. I'd seen like items at a surplus in Eureka, half the price. A pine shelf below the hook board held a nickel revolver and a few bottles of rich booze. All of it stood under a fuzz of dust.

I went to the back and chose a warm twelve of Henry's from behind the fridge glass. On the door handle it said Cool-Rite, and I shook my head at that. Spar rang the beer on his old-time add-up machine. Then he picked up the whiskey and swashed it around like he was makin to take a slug. "This rot ain't fit for glass," he said.

"What's the difference? All ends up in the same place."

He raised his bushies at me. "If I had a taper-corder, I'd play that back for you boys in twenty years. When you'll extinguish between drink and *drink*."

"Drink's drink," Harve said.

"If I had a taper-corder."

"Wouldn't do you no good in no twenty years."

Spar tallied up the whiskey, said, "You're right there, boy." Then he watered up — didn't turn away or nothin — as if he just then got

the drift he was gonna die. "Hell," he said, "I grew up in Somes Bar."
He said that like it explained everything — and it did, too. If you was
me and Harve it sure did. I put ten on the counter and we lit out, left
old Spar to stave off the shivers by himself.

             .

    "You sure put it to him," I said.

    Harve beat the dashboard. "I ain't gonna be around in no twenty
years neither," he said.

    "You'll be —"

    "What?"

    "Nothin."

    "Damn right." He glanced at the clouds that levered up over the
mountains, and bent the rear-view to check his whites. "Feels like I'm
gettin old," he said. "I gotta get a girl." He rubbed his stubble, which
came in thicker on the left side.

    "It'll pass," I said. A mist laid over the road, and rain had started in
the elevations where trees crowded the ravines. Harve switched on the
radio and dialed around. Static.

    "Wish I had a plug," he said. He opened the glove box to empty
chew cans, a few broken smokes and a torn-out centerfold in a plastic
bag. He looked at the picture awhile and shut it back in the box. It was
then we seen the hitcher. She stood at the junction where the old
highway forked into the mountains. I braked and Harve grinned over
at me. I usually slow down to get a hitcher smilin then lean on the
horn and shoot by. But this time I stopped. Hell, the rain.

    "Where do you think I'm goin?" she said before we asked.

    "Any place we take ya," Harve answered.

    She looked both ways and then climbed up. Smelled like she'd
done the yellow in her pants. She had bleached hair that held a perm
curl in patches, blue jeans same as me and Harve, canvas shoes, and a
slicker like the kind road crews wear.

    She held the door open, looked down at the shoulder gravel. "I
didn't move the whole time. Feet was planted," she said.

    Exhaust chuffed into the cab. "Shut the door," Harve said.

    "Lookit them footprints where the rain dint fall. Most hitchers
walk and thumb equal. Not me. Somebody gits you a ride — they'd a
got you a ride back where you was standin in the first place." She shut
the door. We were all three squeezed on the bench seat.

    "Gives," I told her.

    She looked at me dumb and said, "You perfect? You git your diploma?"

"We both got diplomas," Harve said.

"No, I ain't perfect. Hell, I get plenty wrong."

"Shoulda gave her the treatment," Harve said to me.

She laughed. What I learnt early was you talk other then you write, so I gave up the writin part to bear down on talkin.

"The hitcher treatment," Harve said.

"See you boys paid old Spar a visit." She touched the beer box with her shoe. "Stump always creeps me out."

"Creeps is worth it for booze."

"Two a you wouldn't likely be creeps?"

"You're gettin a ride, not a taste."

"Drinkin an shootin," she said. "The fun don't change." She ran her hand along the barrel of my .22 in the overhead rack, looked at her knuckles, and wiped the oil on her jeans. "Least you take good care," she said.

"Sure it changes," I said, thinking of old Spar back there in his shut-down liquor joint. "Fun used to be makin cig lighters outa Jap grenades. Ask Spar."

"That what he lied you? No. He lost his groper in a choker set up north a . . ."

"North a what?"

"North a north. That's the story."

"It was a grenade. WW Two," I said.

"Well, we got inflicting stories then," she said.

I let it drop at that, steered around a road kill and heard her knock against the door. Harve laughed. She pressed the door lock, said, "I got somethin better'n fun, if it clears."

"Looks like she will," I said and hunched on the wheel to get a see at the sky, busted in spots north and all along the granite tops to the east. But in the steeps close by, it kept on, pissed hard.

"I got the inside information," she said. "Pull in back of Jack's. I'll be one minute."

I let the truck idle back of the diner. We cranked the windows against fog-up and caught a good char smell carried down off the kitchen vents by mist. Harve said he could make short work of grub. "Haven't eaten since that weak portion last night," he said. I nodded and kept watch on the back door. It was a back-door kind of day.

When she came runnin out I geared up. She handed Harve a black skillet with a lump of cold grease stuck to the side like it'd been spooned there. She jumped in and we spit gravel through some early green thistle and onto the highway again.

"You got that pretty quick," I said.

"Hell, I worked enough spoons to know where a frypan's kept, and lard."

"D'you steal it?" Harve asked.

"Me? We," she said. "You two are my accomplishes."

We went north out of the drizzle, into the high-ups where wind drove the wet from the road, and the sun brighted up the softwoods.

"I ain't gonna be dropped on no skid for a fry pan and grease," Harve said.

"You won't be, for that."

"Hell," he said, "what's this all about?"

"Hang left," she said to me. "Take it all the way up. Might not be about nothin."

It was a logger road, deep-grooved and packed hard by the heavy trucks. There were washouts where run-off sprung out the mountain-side. Trees marked with orange plastic ribbon stood ten to the mile. Light shot through the mesh of branches and played on the windshield. On sharp turns, the road opened onto a deep gorge, mostly logged out and coming back with buck brush and saps. The saps bright green against the brush.

"Purty country," the hitcher said and tugged at her jeans crotch.

It was something my own ma used to say. "Purty country," just like that. "You got kids?" I asked.

"Kids happens — everybody happens kids."

"Where'd they get to?"

"Fosters mostly. I seen one over in Eureka with some rich old —. Better off, I guess."

"Wouldn't say that," Harve said.

"Yeah, what would you know about it?"

Harve was quiet. He stared out the window on the slope side where a lot of dead needles piled up by the road.

"Oh," she said.

The next washout scarred too deep to pass. I let off the gas and then cut the engine and Harve and me got out and drank two beers apiece standin on the road. The hitcher sat in the cab, smoked a broken from the glove box. Sunlight beamed through in patches, flashed on the muddy water runnin at the bottom of the wash. It had cleared up and gotten colder with wind gusts. We musta been near five thousand feet, if not past.

Through a cut in the trees a buzzard swung a wide arc, and I felt the lift in my gut you always feel when you look down on a flyin bird. Harve popped his knuckles. "Out of range," I said.

"Overshoot," he said and patted his shirt pocket. I heard the dull metal on metal of the .22 shells.

The hitcher leaned forward so I could unrack the rifle. She lit one broken cig with the end of another. Before I went back to Harve she looked at me like she knew everything about me. But she couldn't say nothin — this far in and the keys in my pocket.

"Turn in," Harve said. He shouldered the stock and closed one eye. The buzzard rode a current far out of range and then drew up level with the road, tilted back, and held steady against the wind. Harve sighted for a while and then pushed the safety catch. "Only thing that eats buzzards is more buzzards," he said and shrugged.

"Truck won't go it," I said when the hitcher came over. She grunted and went down the wash, jumped the water, and scrambled up the other side, holdin the skillet in her two hands. I noticed her hips but didn't feel no stir, and she hiked up past the road verge and into the woods. I said, "Harve, we're close."

"Close to nothin," Harve said, but he racked the .22 and got the beer anyway, and we struck out after her, bottles makin music in the cardboard.

We caught up on a bare-ass hump of granite. "All right, boys," she said. "There's our tarn." She wheezed a little and Harve gave her a beer which she guzzled. She put the empty back in the box, took up the pan, and picked her way over boulders to a trail that switch-backed to the little nothin of a lake. I thought, *Hell, I trust this hitcher. She'll show us somethin.* Harve musta likewise. Every time she stopped and took a listen and scanned the sky, he stopped too and checked the ridges, though he couldn'ta known what for.

We came down on the south shore. The lake looked bigger up close, and the wind skimmed off it, pocked the surface. You could see where the pocks started halfway across and rippled at us. "How about the leeward?" I said and gestured to the low cliff that rose up off a beach on the other side.

She shook her head no. "Git a stack for fire," she said and laid the pan on a good flat granite where a campfire had burned before.

Harve polished another beer and then I knocked one back, and we set about to gather wood. "Hell," Harve told me, "a few times I woulda chewed that lard for lack a better." He made a shelf of his arms and I

9

loaded it with hemlock deadfall, scratched all the wood from under
trees where the rains didn't wet it.

"Boys," the hitcher called, "that's plenty."

Harve grinned at me over his stack. He was sweating. "She's callin
us boys," he said.

"Wind got the first match," she said. "Crowd in here." She brought
out the book and struck another match and it flared and went out
before it touched the twig pile. Wind shunted off the lake and made
song over the mouths of our empty bottles. We opened three more.
"Crowd in," she said again. We got down on our knees and hugged into
a lee. I counted three more matches and picked up Harve's odor
through his shirt. Old beer and gamy venison, though we hadn't had
deer since October. She got it lit and the twig pile took off. We added
wood. The song in our bottles went lower fast.

The hitcher took off her road crew slicker, spread it on the ground,
anchored it with four rocks. She had a plain white T-shirt on, thin, the
lace of her bra showing underneath where it clung. Seeing it didn't
move me none. She stoked the fire so the flames licked. Harve sat
down and smiled and opened another. "We gonna pretend?" His voice
came out slow. He leered at the hitcher. "Don't mean ta scare you bout
the treatment," he said. "One foster fed us squash from his garden.
Made us all say, *thank you for the steak*, . . . then to the social."

"Bastard," the hitcher said.

"Yeah," said Harve. He turned away as if from the smoke.

"Quiet now," she said and reached over to Harve. Then she raised
her chin to the sound of a plane, low and steady, far behind the ridge. I
dropped wood on the fire. Sparks jumped.

She yelled, "They always miss this lake by half!" Harve and me got
to our feet. The plane crested the ridge, heavy-bottomed as a fire
bomber, but not as wide. And the hitcher started cursin in a happy
way, and shoutin over the noise about no pretendin, no pretends today.
The plane dipped low over the lake — as low as it could with the cliff
there juttin sharp — and it loosed a hatch near the back, let out a
spray cloud. Then its shadow crossed and the engines rasped overhead,
and I saw the spray thin out and spangle in the sun before it rained
down over the lakeshore and the camp.

Inch-long rainbows flipped in the camp dirt, and on the grass by the
lake, and stuck in the hemlock needles. Harve was swearin and the hitcher
whoopin like July fourth come early. She got out of her shirt, stretched it
over her elbows and fists, and sieved around in the lake shallows.

She took twenty at a time that way. They lolled on the surface, stunned. Harve took five at a time in his hands and brought them down to the water and rinsed off the dirt. I raked them out of the hemlocks and picked clean ones off the bare granite. They smelled the way fresh trout always does, like metal deep back in your nostrils.

The hitcher divvied up the flamin logs from the coals and set the skillet down on the red hots. The lard slid, went to liquid clear and billowed smoke. "Guts doin flips!" Harve said. He sucked a deep breath. When the lard boiled, the hitcher dropped in a trout and it spat into the fire. I watched it turn black.

"Ready," she said and lifted the slicker up by the corners, brought it to the lip of the pan, and tipped one side so they cachéd in at once. She did all this in her bra, blue veins under skin, and the tops of her nipples showin. She stirred the fish with a stick from the wood pile and with the same stick dragged the skillet off the coals and poured off the hot fat which spread over the dirt.

There musta been two hundred trout curled up like popcorn, golden colored. The hitcher jabbed the stick to break up where they clustered. Then she reached into her jeans pocket and brought out a fistful of salt. She bowed her head as if to pray. She was quiet though. We were all quiet. First I looked at the top of her head where the dark roots of her hair showed beneath the bleached. Then I looked at her hand with the salt leakin between her fingers, and felt a rigid calm about it all. The way you feel on days you can't miss with a rifle. I knew she'd finish her prayer, or maybe just her thoughts, and drop that good salt, cover those trout.

* * *

I should tell you, this all took place where the Sierra sort of spins out and skids west into the Marbles, in the north foothill country, where the steelhead still run in numbers. The kind of country, purty country, that keeps its own. Kids born get old around here, and die around here. Like Spar McHugh, who this started off to be about. He ended up drivin off the road up near Somes, about the same time we dug into those trout. The next day it turned warm and the buzzards marked his truck. The bi-weekly called it an accident, but it's the way some of us go. I said this started to be about Spar McHugh. And I guess it was.

Linda Watanabe McFerrin

The Dojo — Lesson 1

Just beyond her reach
the movement hung
precise as a Kanji character,
as meticulous in execution.

Every day she labored toward it,
arms reaching,
traced its reflection.

Sometimes she'd touch a lower corner.
She could fly,
the movement when she caught it,
effortless.

The instructor muttered, "higher."
The redness in her face betrayed
"wrong-thinking."   •
Her desire only made her thirsty.

Linda Watanabe McFerrin

Sakura-no-sono

It was early spring in your uncle's cherry orchard,
blossoms — pink.
The last time you were there, you
wore high heels
for the first time —
just sixteen.

This time you were running.
The raw cold, drawn in
with every breath,
a knife blade driving
deep into your chest.
Nose bleeding from the effort,
you tasted salt.

And all around you, the cherry orchard
was ablaze,
a maze of black-trunked trees
like torches dipped in rags and oil
and lit.

American bombers whined overhead,
fat insects swarming.
Your arms, like skinny leather wings,
cranked at your sides.
You ran, earth-tethered, knees shaking.

And you saw the man beside you running, headless,
30 yards before
he fell as you
were running
on and on
toward an invisible finish line.

And the branches of the cherry trees were lit
with flames,
the sparks — petals of fire, carried
on the wind.

Legacy

I.

In the first act, remember her madness —
her wide gash of sorrow, her *obi* of blood?
The tragic kabuki heroine,
she committed *seppuku*,
hid the cross-wise cut
under mulberry robes.

We walked like *obakes*, like unsettled ghosts.
She cut my long hair. It frightened her.
It stole the first scene of the play.
She made me wear wooden clogs.
She plucked out my eyebrows,
so that people would mistake me for the moon.

II.

In the second act, she unwound her *obi* of blood
and wrapped it around me,
tied my hands and my ankles.
Not even my weeping could wipe it away,
could bring her back from the realm of the dead
where she's wandered as long as I've known her.
She said, "We should all have died at once.
We should lie in a common grave."

III.

In the third act, she made and unmade me,
told me again of her deep, bitter wound,
said, "This is your legacy, daughter.
Let the anger boil up inside you,
let the red pour from your ears and your eyes."
She drained me of color and sutured my heart.
I rang like a bell. "Sorrow. Sorrow."

IV
In the fourth act, the psychiatrist entered.
I thanked him and gave him black stones.
I added them to the scales on his desk.
I discovered that none of his patients survived.
"Look," I said, "I'm better."
"Yes," he said. "Let's pretend."

Epilogue.
In the epilogue, I am walking along a seashore.
I'm pretending that beauty can reach me.
I've thrown out the kimonos, the costumes and robes.
I've made a new self out of flowers and surgical steel,
a shiny new self that blooms every spring.
And I've cast all the ancestors
back over the sea
like pearls.
They are pain.
They are sand.

Gary Cooke

The Road Between Them

This kind of country
makes your heart spill.
Wildflowers everywhere,
a sign saying
Sweet Medicine Ranch.

Just below Latrobe,
the dark eyes of a mare
disturb you, until the curve
in the road lets you see the horse
on the other side, head down
in the long grass.

The road between them
wet and dark, a sky purple
with thunder, you feel something like love,
even driving by,
big drops of rain splashing
like tears on the windshield.

Poem Found on a Riverbank

Her soul is the color
of the dark iris,
folded upon itself and
hanging
just beneath the earth.

One morning her eyes
will turn blue
and the orange
she peels for breakfast
will be a butterfly.

Her hair will lift
in the wind,
like the gulls that rise
on one wing and
make slow circles.

She will open her lips
to sing
and the whole river
will spill out.

The Soft Spot

"God is not a woman," Frenchy said. "I know this because if she were, we'd wake up every two months and find the planets all rearranged."

"That's not fair and you know it," Crystal fumed. "You make jokes about God because you can't handle change, that's all."

"Change? I can't handle tripping over furniture, that's what I can't handle. Christ, I'm black and blue!"

Crystal turned and walked away, her black pumps angry at him all the way down the hall.

"If you had your way every stick of furniture in this house would be nailed to the floor, and I'd be nailed to the floor, too," she called back when she reached the bedroom door. The last thing Frenchy saw was the flip of her long, dark hair and a flash from her new eyeglasses. It reminded him of the tracer bullets you saw in smudged films about World War II.

Frenchy looked around to find a place to sit. Crystal had moved the loveseat to the far wall, under the large mirror, and his reading chair to the other side of the fake fireplace. He flopped his length into the reading chair hoping to find something familiar in the room, at least. Then he saw that she'd taken the reading lamp and put it where it would spill its little puddle of light onto the telephone table, which used to be at one end of the couch.

Frenchy gently cupped his long fingers and held both hands over his eyes, his elbows resting on the arms of the chair. With his green, deep-set eyes thus covered, and the tip of his long, straight nose obscured, he was reduced to sweeping waves of darkish hair that looked like they had been combed on the head of a doll by a child. His impossibly long legs were splayed in front of him. He was in his thinking posture.

Despite their reasonably long courtship, Frenchy had never noticed any compulsion in Crystal to play furniture like pieces of chess. As a single woman, she had never once to his knowledge moved more than the vases of flowers she kept changing every Saturday morning. Maybe the bells that had clanged over their heads at the wedding somehow activated some soft part of her brain that governed interior decorating.

It started out with her tossing little blankets onto the arms and backs of chairs.

"Those are throws," she explained to him. "They give the room a casual look."

"They look more like something that's been left," he told her. "Shouldn't they be folded? Shouldn't they just be stacked up and issued during cold weather like the way the Red Cross does it?"

That was the first time he'd discovered that Crystal's eyes were not really garden soil brown the color of mud puddles, but more like hard-packed clay, fired to withstand for centuries the march of civilization across the most arid parts of the earth.

"Honey," he said to her about a year into the marriage, "are you unhappy? Is that why you're always changing things around in here?"

Crystal had given him her "I'm counting to 10 before I answer" gaze and then uttered her response, in her finest kindergarten teacher voice.

"Happiness has nothing to do with it."

Frenchy had never understood what that meant. He still didn't.

His memories were interrupted by muffled scuffs and chattering pushes coming from down the hall.

"Crystal!" he cried out, launching himself out of the chair with a series of angular moves. Frenchy dashed down the long hallway, carefully, almost dancingly — swinging his hips left and right to avoid the new umbrella stand and the three empty pedestals that used to display the busts of dead composers.

Breathing hard, he placed his ear against the bedroom door.

"I hear you out there," she said accusingly.

Frenchy could have sworn it was the voice of a parrot — the same stabbing sort of inflections.

"Sweetheart, can I come in and talk?"

"You don't talk, you just criticize."

Frenchy had faced similar charges in the past. His mind raced for a response.

"I can hear you moving things and I just wondered if I can help," he said. He felt her silence. Help her! He'd never felt so brilliant. He could sense her straightening her back and standing still, her head cocked toward the door.

"Do you mean that?"

"Of course I mean it," he said. Frenchy took a step away from the door. There was a lovely little click. For some reason it reminded him of how it felt undoing the first button on a silky blouse when he knew the woman wearing it was not going to stop him.

Frenchy entered the room with all the professionalism of a police detective, his eyes doing a quick sweep as he calmly approached his petite wife, who was even shorter now that she'd kicked off her angry shoes. The dresser was gone, as far as he could tell, and the foot of the bed was at a 45-degree angle from the south wall.

"I was just reading today about how important it is to align your bed with the natural flow of universal forces," Crystal said. "I think the bed ought to go this way."

She indicated "this way" with a sweep of her right hand. Frenchy noticed she'd gone back to her frightening red fingernail polish. As he followed her sweep he caught a glimpse of the dresser, which she'd somehow managed to shove to the wall between the closet and the bathroom.

"Honey, I worry about your doing this all by yourself," Frenchy said in his kindly doctor voice. "You could hurt yourself."

"Well, you get so upset when I move things. I'm afraid to ask you."

"Ask me, sweetheart," Frenchy said.

"Oh, Frenchy," Crystal said, resting her forehead now against his chest in what was the first display of affection he'd seen in weeks.

Frenchy lowered his face and kissed the top of her head, his lips aware of the silky texture of her hair, his nose flaring slightly at the faint scent of something flower-like and wistful. He kissed her again and again, those wedding bells clanging in his head, hoping to find the soft spot he knew was there — unless, God help him, she had moved it.

Steve Wilson

Meditation on Birds Near Nightfall

Near last light, no sounds but the breeze
through leaves in the sycamores.
Above, there's a sudden curve of birds —

crows — dark against the blue white
sky. As they pass, their wings slip through
air — the sound of skin brushing skin.

Five, now six, heavy vultures rise
upon thermals edging a spring front.
A few falcons, smaller, glide among them.

They're different. *Stream*-lined.
The quick angle of wing. Slendered bodies
that thin down to tails fanned open

to catch the current. They follow the warm,
circling on flows, while down here, evening
cool is coming. It's a final call from winter,

miles north now, that grows and spirals through
dark saying *listen*, until light's too little
to see. Settled, even the songbirds fall silent.

Belden Johnson

Encounter Group

when diane cries I want to hug her
  but I don't because
    demetria is watching
& when demetria cries I want to hug her
  but I don't because
    diane is watching
& when demetria hugs diane & they cry together
  I feel wet wings feathering my eyecorners
    & I want to hug them
but I don't
  because
    they might misinterpret it
& when leroy finally goes across to hug them
  I decide it's all right
    to do a little hug
but first
  I put on
    my shoes

Jeff Kane

Karma Sierra #112, Guns Don't Kill People

Yuba's nearest neighbor up the canyon, Wesson Smith, was a longtime
loner who tended a barn full of weapons and a litany of grudges.
Wesson was the sort of man about whom the neighbors say, afterward,
"Well, he was a nice guy, kind of kept to himself."

One Friday morning Yuba ran into Wesson on the road. He flashed
him his customary V sign. "Hey," Yuba called, "love is everywhere."

"Yeah, right," Wesson grunted. "Heard you're gonna patch these
potholes."

"Yeah, Saturday, as a matter of fact," Yuba replied. "Are you gonna
come out and help?"

Wesson rested his hand on his holster. "Are you kidding? I don't
know who's gonna be out here. Could be anybody. Tell 'em not to
come by my place if they don't want lead poisoning. I got a license for
this, y'know, and I can protect my private property."

"Hey, whatever," Yuba said. "Cool. I'll see to it nobody comes up."

That night, Yuba heard Wesson empty his six-shooter into the side
of his hill, followed by his shotgun and finally some kind of automatic.
Recalling that Wesson often target-practiced after downing a bottle or
two of apple wine, Yuba began to wonder how safe his neighborhood
was. He phoned the Sheriff's department.

"Ah, I was wondering if there's anything I can do about my
neighbor who fires his weapons all the time?"

"Do?" asked the dispatcher. "What do you want to do? What's the
problem?"

"The problem? Well, the noise, for one thing."

"He's got a right to fire his weapons. Don't you fire your weapons?"

"All I've got is a slingshot."

"Get a .22. It's great for dispatching varmints. You'll love it."

"Well, what if he shoots this direction?"

"If he hits anybody, then you phone us. Till then, he hasn't broken
any laws."

Yuba's exchange with the dispatcher didn't do much to settle his fears. That Saturday, he and his neighbors filled the road's potholes but, continually imagining their heads in Wesson's crosshairs, stopped a few yards short of his property line.

The following day was the spring equinox, and neither Wesson nor anyone else was going to dampen Yuba's celebration. He broke out a few bottles of his homemade root beer and found a string of Chinese firecrackers he'd scored in the big city.

It turned out to be a beautiful afternoon. Yuba stuffed himself on leftover tempeh enchiladas and danced in the clearing to his own harmonica. As the sun set, he laid out his firecrackers.

The millisecond after he lit their fuse, though, something told Yuba this might not be a smart thing to do. The staccato blasts echoed through the canyon, followed by a resounding silence.

Then Yuba heard one more firecracker, but from up the hill. Then came another and another. He realized Wesson must be shooting, and he was shooting because he'd interpreted Yuba's fireworks as his own personal Waco, an assault on his sacred property by heavy-handed, hobnailed feds. Following the next report Yuba heard a hiss over his head, and a thud as the bullet slammed into the oak behind him.

He gawked at the shuddering tree, then back up the hill, ran into his house and quickly phoned 911.

"Hey," he breathily greeted the Sheriff's dispatcher. "My neighbor's firing at me."

"How do you know?"

"Because one, he's a notorious gun freak, two, he's shooting right now, and three, I just heard one fly near my head."

"Has he hit anyone?"

"No, not yet, but if he kills me, I won't be able to phone you back."

"No need to get snotty, sir. We can't get involved until a law's been broken, and until now, from what you tell me, everyone's still safe."

Yuba stared at his phone as slugs buzzed like furious wasps over his roof.

"Sir? Are you all right?"

"No, I'm not all right. Bullets are everywhere."

"Sir, another call's coming in. Is there anything more you need to tell me?"

Yuba made a critical decision. "Ahhhh, yes," he said. "Um, ah, I need to tell you this: I think . . . I think he's on drugs."

"Did you say drugs?" The dispatcher's voice suddenly took on an edge.

"Yeah, I think he's high on something, if you know what I mean. Says he takes it for his arthritis."

The dispatcher said, "Okay, I'll need your name and address, please."

At three o'clock the following morning, two dozen armor-plated ninjas kicked down Wesson's door. The deputies found no intoxicants other than apple wine, but they had to arrest Wesson for assaulting one of their number.

Later that day, the Sheriff himself phoned Yuba. "Thanks for the tip," he said. "We didn't find his stash, but I've had my eye on that van of his for some time. I'd be surprised if my boys didn't find something in it and we have to confiscate it."

"Well, as long as justice prevails," Yuba replied. "Love is everywhere."

Karma Sierra #77, Chock Full of Fiber

Richard arrived at River Song on time and scanned the dining room for Marianne. She wasn't there yet, but he did recognize most of the diners as local psychotherapists who, he knew, practiced mainly on one another. It reminded him of an African village he'd heard about in which each household made its living doing its neighbor's laundry. As Richard removed his hat and perused the daily specials chalkboard, he felt a tap on his shoulder.

He turned. "Marianne!" he exclaimed, hugging her. "How've you been?"

"Terrific!" she replied perkily. "It's this stuff I'm taking."

"Oh, yeah? What?"

"AmeriVite."

"Amer . . ."

"AmeriVite," Marianne repeated.

"Cool!" Richard exclaimed, sounding ferociously positive.

The hostess wafted up to them. "Two?" Her tie-dyed aura swayed gently as she led them to a table and sat them down.

"The special today is the tempeh burrito," she softly crooned, handing them menus. She smiled beatifically, exhaled with a wistful sigh, drew a long inspiration, and continued. "It comes on a sprouted wheat tortilla, five ninety-five. Please take your time." She floated away, angel down on a summer breeze.

Richard laid his hat in his lap. "Tell me again, Marianne. Ameri . . .?"

"AmeriVite. Balanced vitamins and minerals. Organic sources, bioenergized. I've become a distributor, along with everyone in my women's group."

Richard leaned back and smiled. "Well, a distributor! Me, too."

"No!" Marianne beamed radiantly. "AmeriVite?"

"Well, no, as a matter of fact. Biozyme."

At the adjacent table, Shivalingam set down his gluten calzone, swallowed and leaned toward their table. "Biozyme?" he asked. "I hear you say Biozyme?"

"Yeah, Biozyme," Richard answered. "Harmonized blend of phytonutrients."

"Hey, tell me about it," Shivalingam chuckled. "I was a Level Four Associate. It cured my Environmental Sensitivity."

"Awesome," Richard said. "Cured my candida allergy."

The waitress materialized. "Hi," she said sweetly. "My name is Saccharinanda, and I'll be your server today." Regarding Richard and Marianne with the eyes of a young doe, she asked, "Have you decided what you'd like? We're offering complimentary AmeriVite tablets with lunch today."

Marianne grinned to Richard. "See? Sells itself."

"Well, I'll tell you," the waitress testified, "it sure restored my homeostasis. I can get you a great deal on your first three months."

Marianne said, "I'll try the tofu quiche, with a milk thistle smoothie."

Richard pinched his lips as he ran his finger down the menu. "Hm. I'll have the turnip stroganoff, I think, and a Spirulina spritzer. But none of those tablets, though. You're not supposed to mix Biozyme with any supplements."

Saccharinanda rolled her eyes skyward, silently mouthing "supplements." She wrote the rest of the order and disappeared into the kitchen.

Shivalingam leaned toward them once again. "Biozyme's okay," he continued, "but I just learned something about it."

Suddenly you could've heard a pinch of saffron hit River Song's floor. Every diner leaned toward Shivalingam as though he were Moses about to read from the tablets. He whispered, "Biozyme's Co-Q10 neutralizes its B-17. But you can get around it by popping organic selenium."

A gasp resounded through the room, crescendoed to a buzz and all present realized they'd read about this next week in the *Gold Valley Jungian*.

Richard visibly paled but quickly recentered himself. "Well," he countered, "you're talking about standard Biozyme, not Biozyme Plus™, which happens to contain selenium."

Shivalingam, no less pleased with himself, shrugged and returned to his calzone. "Hey, whatever," he conceded.

Richard turned back to Marianne. "You know, I'd love to loan you my Biozyme audiotape. People share their cure from multiple sclerosis, arthritis, even Peyronie's disease."

Marianne replied, "Tell you what, I'll trade you for my video of people cured of cancer and rheumatism by AmeriVite."

The waitress brought their lunches, along with a small, unendangered hardwood tray that bore Marianne's complimentary AmeriVite tablet. Marianne swallowed the tablet, picked at her tofu quiche. "Not bad," she pronounced, "but I wish they'd use tofu flocked with lime-stone spring water."

"Yeah, too bad about that," Richard replied. "No complaints here, though. Mmmm! This stroganoff's as chock full of fiber as a jute doormat."

After they ate, they walked out to the parking lot, where they traded tapes and one-month supplies of AmeriVite and Biozyme Plus™ and hugged their farewell. Marianne drove off to her escrow company. Richard donned his hat, adjusted his gun belt, got into his patrol car and checked in with the dispatcher. Feeling the comforting swelling of his fibrous lunch, he glowed with gratitude that he lived in such a healthy town.

Dan Bellm

Siren Song

The older hikers are staring into the water —
it looks too hard to get down to it over the rocks —

and the woman tells her husband, it's all right,
she's close enough, she's seen enough,

but she doesn't sound convinced and he knows it, turning away —
he's tired now, but she would like to go further, as I

am going, because I still have strong legs and good boots
she envies, I suppose, almost lured to try, and then

they are gone. It takes me only a minute to clamber down
and ford the swampy inlet, wet to the waist,

and I'm swimming to the raised tip of the dead limb
at the center of Shirley Lake like one preserved past age

in the delicious chill that calls to mind
how geniuses are having their brains frozen now

against a future they trust will remember them
and sigh for their return, but what if

your brain isn't your best feature
or your noblest part, as if even the noblest skull-mass

isn't past useful freeze-drying at the point of death,
shocked too often by blips of logic or passion,

too many of its little brilliancies lost in corridors
like books misfiled in the library and therefore lost.

simply not there? So I wish my legs to be iced up instead
for striding and climbing through as much of time as I am able,

walking ahead of others as I have always left my companions
irritably lagging a yard or so behind

but haven't the bones shifted place themselves
under the sedimentary loosening sway of the spine

and the muscles come unmoored enough under the pubic bone
to make my youth unreturnable to me even in the age

when the cryogenic dead shall be raised incorruptible?
And this is why a pain shot down the leg this morning

as soon as the hiking boot went on: the sorry limb
knew it was being summoned for another test of greatness

and thought about failing graciously with a small thank-you,
staying to recline in the hotel lobby in the valley

stroked by the coffin-like plush of the sofas,
guessing at how it will be to stir inside the box for centuries

whenever the earth contracts and settles
under the compacting entrance of more and more death,

its weakest joint, the sprained V
of its gone sexual exuberance, numbing slightly

at the arrivals of beings it cannot shift or turn to nestle against
because there is always more numbing,

more separation into ever finer dust,
a decomposition as patient as this granite's into the meadow

as I swim back seriously shivering now
to sun myself, naked as a siren on the rock,

one of the immortal beauties, a warning, a temptation,
combing my silvering hair.

Aspens

The individual life is not the point — *admire me*
I am a violet, and so on, as John Keats mocked
in the voice of the self who wants to be more precious
than existence — long parentless by then,
nursing his brother Tom through the long bloodcoughing
months of death and knowing his own could come soon,
perhaps before love, or another visitation of poetry,
though he had only reached the Chamber of Maiden-thought
in the house of many rooms he was sketching out
in his own faint light — *on all sides many doors set open but all*
dark all leading to dark passages — maybe few to be revealed
in an individual life. So the naturalist led us poets
up a creekbed to show us a tiny portion of our own world:
a fragile meetingpoint of volcanic rock & granite
that over a hundred thousand years urged forth a way
for water to wash down and make this canyon to the valley:
told us that the grove of quaking aspens we stopped beside
ought to call into question our definition of a tree:
not separate trees but clones sprung from an underground
rhizomal oh I don't know what the word was,
which makes me ashamed — I didn't write it down — as if
knowledge of the names of things means understanding anything
of what they are — the other poets, I figured, were writing down
notes for me — wanting really to have the labeled placards
in an arboretum (*dote upon me I am a primrose*) so I could
walk away satisfied knowing more than enough but actually
nothing much. The point was that the system of roots beneath us
was vaster than we could think, a million years old or so,
and apparently so capable of continuing sending up clones each season
that it can wait for the arrival of the next ice age to this valley
if it takes another million years, and the theorizers who know
that our minds and words stop short of what this might mean
have posited what they can only call "theoretical immortality."
(All of the poets wrote *that* one down.) All right, so I returned
to poetry so late, guilty, ashamed, regretful, sad, all right.
My teacher beside me — disoriented by all these

lateblooming Sierra wildflowers unknown in northern New Hampshire —
another system but not another earth — connected underneath —
(same late-July mosquitoes here as there biting me though,
taking me back to my summers by Mt. Chocorua at the commie camp,
swimming in the deep pond there, decided to be a writer and so
to change the world, *rich in the simple worship of a day*) — she said
she was grateful there was such a community of writers as this one
and she had found it — so little of the usual mutual hatred
and self-mistrust because we're working every day and facing
the blankness of paper, urging each other on, not showing off our
bundles of poems from home to be doted upon or angling
for career moves, though I do want my fucking book to get out
of my house. She agreed with me, no, you are not, at the age
of 45, the next young thing the poetry biz is waiting
to discover, and you can thank God herself for it, having had
students at the age of 23 all but drown in acclaim and felt
afraid for them as in, O honey — just wait until you're in
a small town somewhere with an underpaying job and a couple of
babies, not enough time, a husband who helps out, or not,
and one book on the shelf while the world has moved on
to the next bright morning star — that's when, if you're lucky,
you'll be a writer. Send down your taproot then, into the
many-chambered whatever it is, the comfort and fright of it,
that we're all connected. *And thus by every germ of Spirit
sucking the Sap from mould ethereal every human might become great,
and Humanity instead of being a wide heath of Furse and Briars
with here and there a remote Oak or Pine, would become
a grand democracy of Forest Trees.* These plant "communities" —
manzanita, huckleberry, snow-something, oh I didn't write those down
either I was so tired, the words are not the point — they're migrating
over geological time — they send messages to each other
across the great spungy rootmass about changes in temp, and
rainfall, outbreaks of blight, accumulated experience we'd call
gossip or history, the sports and weather, film at 11 — they slowly
move, and so others move with them, what's the choice — the point
is the interwoven indistinguishableness that all life feeds
and is fed by, not the individual life. And the hope
that I will be communicated with among the forms of life
must be what is meant by a blessing — say, the man I saw
laying his hands on another man's head, in the rain, to bless him,

in a crowd at the corner of Post & Stockton in the middle of the day —
it must be only our bodies, our skin, that make us think
we are contained in one place in one self, as a tree appears to end
at the root, the rock, the leaf-edge, the air, as a mountain appears
to end at the level ground, so we need the laying on
of hands to make an entryway into the one
oh what will I call it? We don't even have the same desires
as ourselves, as when the ex-President said, "I have opinions
of my own. Strong opinions. But I don't always agree with them."
We are temporary shadows constantly turning around
to misremember, elaborate constructions
unrecoverable a moment later, contradictory lifelines
in the palms of our hands. So even a sad song causes happiness
when it comes from the heart. So Jacob asked a blessing of his father
as I did, though I too had to steal it, holding his hand as he died
in a coma in a narrow bed: still, I think he was waiting for me.
And afterwards we go on living, at our own mercy,
which can be short at hand. Am I too old?
I am not the next young thing but that has never stopped
the subterranean-stream-continuation of all the desires.
Band of rose gold on my finger, and 16 years of marriage
to the man I love, faithful in our "open relationship"
well are we? though openness can be an aperture or chasm. The man
handing me change in the hardware store with my wall-grabbers
and wingnuts had two nipple rings, which I thought was one
too many, and was young enough to be my child; he made me hot
as our hands met though it meant nothing much, and am I too old
to get a nipple ring? I want to ask him if I did that would it
hurt, but a part of me I love is afraid it might not hurt enough:
more unfulfillment in desire, even the desire for pain, which runs on
in the underground stream, and resurfaces each season
in its fashion, as here in a brightly-lit store midday
on Castro St.: I wanted to lick the salt from his skin.
Oh what would I turn into if I were single again? The devious
frightened loner I was before. Undiscovered by poetry.
Now we look upward on the trail because the life of birds,
living or ornamental, this one or the birds of tapestry in the decor
of our minds, the nothing that is not there, and the nothing
that is — their life is song. A junco but I didn't see it,
the guide helped us notice and then I heard it, a scold, a

trailing-off *compleynt*, as Bela Bartók must have heard
the actual Hungarian birds of his youth that he lived among
before the disaster of our midcentury dispersed the forms of life
but how did he still hear them and place them
directly by their song and without names into that never-quite-
finished Piano Concerto No. 3, his cry of anguished love
and a capitulation before some wellspring he knew would continue
after him, or at any rate that's what I heard when I first
heard it in Ann Arbor some twenty years ago, the days when I
was almost giving up on my own soul and living in that piss-
smelling boarding house on Miller Avenue, mourning my first lover,
smoking so much dope, back in the closet again,
romanticizing Larry and Sadie the drunks from the U. P. next door
because they were Indians and had done so much Real Time
in the Washtenaw County Jail right across the street —
we heard the screams and fighting of the prisoners at night —
and who therefore seemed to live more intensely, have *more* life,
than one such as me writing term papers on *Middlemarch*,
when what I wanted from them really was another sedative drug —
what a sorrowful young youth I was, pitiful jade plant in my window
likewise half in love with death, but I had a rainsoaked *Book of*
Nightmares and *A Love Supreme* and the birds that Bela Bartók
conjured up for me, one mortal body passing the song on to another
across indefinite time, his final music, so full of legend and glory,
sitting on a cot an almost penniless refugee in 1945 on W. 57th St.
in New York knowing he was dying, racing to leave it
as a birthday present for his wife and even more, a useful
concert-piece that she could go on playing and earn a little
money from to make her way, the sheet music found only later
lying out of order on every available surface of bed and desk
and floor, a windowless room in which he caused
the birds of gone-forever Hungary to go on singing.

Thekla Clemens

The Promise

This is not an easy place to love —
like the body, it can be deceptive,
lush curves of the coastal range,
refuge for gray fox and small towns,
funky splendor of San Francisco,
vast expanse of the Sacramento delta,
the cruel innocence of the desert.

And over everything the clear and golden light,
defying smog,
blessing even the billboard signs
hovering
over the crowded avenues,
the palm trees on Dolores Street,
lending new angles to the tired faces of Russian immigrants
waiting for the bus on the corner of Geary and 19th.

My husband and I had too much of the same hunger,
a need like a wound;
we could not fill each other.

Ten years I watched the hills turn green and brown,
followed rippled folds into canyons of seasonal creeks,
feasted on the orange of the poppy,
cried into the cloudless blue.

When I left,
I moved to the foothills
away from the crowds,
a place with hard soil, dry and cracked
like the soles of an old woman's feet,
with smooth madrones, twisted manzanitas,
the river a shape shifter, its force moving boulders, constantly
changing course, its color.

I have come to this place, the house I bought,
as to a true marriage,
and we have held our promise,
kept each other safe.

And over everything the light
like hope,
it surrounds me always,
not an element,
but a memory,
more ephemeral than the air that makes it visible.
As necessary as silence.
In each ray,
the conquered darkness.

Carol Wade Lundberg

Canyon

At first you lay
a shallow trough
on the belly
of your mother
looking upward through
seas fingered
with dim light
and the rhythmic dance
of cells

How long you slept
with what strange lullabies
of air and wave
we have imagined
with finite wonder

Beyond our limited awe
that slow
torquing birth
your warm sea cradle
flowing down

still wet rock
limbs exposed to stoic shapers
of gravity and light

your adolescent journey
through layers
of yielding
and confrontation
toward a remembered
sea home

Carol Wade Lundberg

In dreams we
travel inward toward
those wet beginnings
Invisible gills
inhale a common truth

All journeys
are like this

Ross Drago

Across the Street

I was introduced to the works of Shakespeare in a curious way. When I was thirteen, a woman moved into the apartment house across the street. The large Victorian Buffalo house had been misused for many years. It was not an Italian family home, where parents lived downstairs and newly married daughter and son-in-law took a flat upstairs. People came and went. The lawn was worn to flat mud by men who took car parts, cleaned them with kerosene, and then left town.

The old gray apartment house had a great verandah, as it was called, a porch with a roof, supported by ionic wooden columns carved and fluted and, as with the rest of Buffalo, painted brown or gray. Stairs that were quite wide led up to the porch, and on it was a large rocking couch, called a glider.

The woman who moved in looked mad. She was old, perhaps in her late seventies, and she had carrot-orange hair that came out in a wild and thick shock and leapt, even plunged, down her back like a waterfall. It splashed in every direction, and she wore a bright pink housecoat, tied at the waist.

This woman had a tiny face, relative to her hair. Her lips were painted red, and her cheeks were an equal intensity of extreme red rouge. When from our picture window I saw her on the porch, walking back and forth, talking to herself, I asked my mother about her. My mother said that she had been an actress. That was all she said.

Every day she would come early to the porch, with a cup of tea or coffee, and begin her endless soliloquy. As it was summer and I was not in school, I would stand in our living room and watch her through the front window. I imagined that she spoke the lines of William Shakespeare. I had never read Shakespeare nor seen him played. I therefore imagined lines that were the greatest verse that I could imagine. I became addicted to watching her deliver her lines and imagining what each sentence was as it fell from her overly painted lips. I fell in love with her, and with all of the works of Shakespeare, as I imagined them to be.

In this way I became her avid audience. I imagined what she looked like when she was young. She smoked cigarettes, walked impatiently back and forth on the Plymouth Avenue stage, and played the words in my mind with sudden stops, wild gestures, and then calming finality. I was a deaf man at the world's greatest play. I knew then that theater made sense to me.

Held together like a tension structure, she was as thin as a person could be, yet vibrating like cords that were too tight. All that held her together was the tension of these thinnest lashings. Her body had been converted over into almost pure soul. It was snapped this way and that as her spirit flicked it across the porch. She was amazing to me.

It was at the height of summer that an elderly gentleman moved into the apartment. My mother informed me that he was a retired fireman. Indeed, this square, earthy man still wore the dark blue uniform of a fireman. Over his dark blue pants and shirt, he also wore a gray mailman's sweater, so that he was an odd combination of many social services. He had thick black hair and was very cleanly shaven.

It took no time in the stuffy, hot apartment house for these two to bring their coffee or their tea to the front porch and sit on the top of the steps, side by side, quietly talking.

She was all electric, aflame, and he was an old fireplace. They had a million things to say to one another. It was as though two lifetimes had been lived solely for the sake of these conversations, lives lived solely as preparation for these summer afternoons on the porch.

I would watch them both now, and in my mind, I could hear his soft voice, telling her things he knew for sure, without a doubt, and how this must have hypnotized her, to be with a man who knew what he knew for certain, when all of her life had been made of what-if's and could-it-be's.

And so the summer was spent, the retired fireman and the actress on the glider, now holding hands, sipping tea, talking the entire day, day after day.

It was in fall, when the maple tree that I loved had already been shocked once more by the sudden change, and her leaves were red like the woman across the street, that the bells in the firehouse down the street rang three times. I knew the firemen, all of them, and Mike especially, and I knew that when the bell rang three times it meant firehouse number three.

A man rolled the fire door upward with a crank and the small engine sang the song that made my dog Corky lay back his head and slowly howl.

"Corky, stop!" my mother said.

The fire truck started its siren and instead of flying out the great doorway and down Jersey Street, it made an awkward and slow turn and came, wrong way, down Plymouth Avenue's one-way street.

The fire truck stopped at the house across the street and three men wheeled a gurney inside. I watched it being carried up the stairs in the dark apartment house. In a while they appeared carrying the retired fireman, and an ambulance arrived from the other direction. They wheeled him into the ambulance, and sirens began again as they moved slowly around and back down the narrow street.

The old fireman never came back to Plymouth Avenue. The woman with the bright orange hair came out onto the porch the next morning. I could see that she had changed as she stood on the porch. She did not sit on the steps. She did not sit on the glider. She could only stand on the porch with the flat mud patch and look out, as if on a darkened stage. She had been like the E string on a violin. She had been wound too tight. Now, this final turning had increased the tension higher still, sounding a note that was beyond my ability to hear.

Waiting for the Bank to Open

In Buffalo, outside the restaurant, the fine snow hissed by the window. I would have to wait another half-hour before the downtown main bank opened. I asked Dorothy for a refill of coffee. I had finished a glazed twist donut, and although I was still hungry, I had only thirty cents left in my pocket.

Dorothy was thin and her hair was straight, turning gray from dark brown. Her eyes were Italian, but she was not. They had darkness beneath them, and in her eyes, like stage suns with still lashes thick from mascara, there was a sadness I hated to see.

Her skin was getting soft looking. I had touched a young woman once, a woman I didn't know, accidentally. I was walking behind her, and my hand grazed her rear end, and for the first time I felt a woman's softness in a sexual way. But that kind of softness was different from the way Dorothy's skin looked like it might feel. It was beginning to look too soft, as though she were leaving. It was starting to look like flesh whose spirit was quietly and over time slipping away.

She poured my coffee. I studied her hand, took a picture of her wrist with my mind. When she had gone to talk with the older woman at the other end of the counter, I took out my sketchpad and pencil and drew her hand. I called it, "At the Deco Restaurant this morning, Dorothy poured."

Funny there was no low society magazine, like there were high society ones. There were so many people who ate here, and no one ever covered it except an artist or two. I entertained the idea of starting a low society magazine, interviewing people who had donuts and coffee every morning at the Deco Restaurant. How did they like their coffee? Did they use a napkin last Wednesday when they had guests? Who did they meet here? What were they wearing for lunch? Did they have lunch? Where did they buy their hat? For how much? How did they arrive? The more I thought it out, the more I liked the idea. It would be the first society magazine that read like *The Grapes of Wrath*.

Last week it had turned into 1957. Everyone knew it was going to do that, but still, what a surprise! They celebrated it as if it had had a choice about whether to happen. What luck! To celebrate in spring, because you survived the winter, that seemed like a reasonable surprise. What luck! But to celebrate what was inevitable seemed strange to me.

I drank my coffee slowly. I did not want to be outside waiting for the bank to open. My buckle boots were holding melting snow, dripping on the footrest beneath the counter. Long underwear, white, thermo type, absorbed water upward like a slow wick on my ankles, and I wore double socks over still-cold feet. My long gray wool coat was too thin, and two sweaters were not enough to stop that wind from blowing through me, making me unbearably sexually aroused. It didn't happen often, but on occasion there was a wind that seemed magnetic. It was that wind that could not be stopped. From nowhere, always in winter, it came through my body like a violin bow across a violin, and I wanted to stop and wail at the feeling of sexuality. There was no hiding from it. It was blowing through the restaurant. It was after me.

In ten more minutes the main bank in Buffalo would open. For some reason I remembered a day when my mother had brought me downtown to the bank. I was ten. She took me not to the tellers but to the carpeted area of the enormous, cathedral-like building. She introduced me to the president of the main bank. It never struck me as being odd, we being so terribly poor, that she should know the president. He welcomed her, called her Frances, and shook my little hand.

All of that I guess was important to her. She had gone through the Depression. She never recovered from it. Security meant everything to her after that, economic security. She had bonds. War bonds. They looked like giant money. They looked important. They were safe, she told me. You could trust them. Clearly, you could trust nothing else. What a great mystery it all was to me, all of the important paper things. The important paper work in my life was all made up in sketchpads. Mine said Drago, in a quick scrawl; hers said Alexander Hamilton and Benjamin Franklin and Ulysses S. Grant. Who could compete with the already known?

I made another sketch of Dorothy passing by with a box of napkins in her hand and signed it Ulysses S. Grant. It definitely took on another air. Suddenly, my work looked valuable.

In two minutes they would open the door to the bank. I gave Dorothy my money at the register and left a fifteen-cent tip. The coffee and the donut were thirty-five cents. That left me fifty cents. It added up, they said. Fifteen cents, a couple of times a day from me alone, eventually amounted to something. I knew they must be right.

I shoved my hands into my gloves and my gloves into my pockets and went out into the icy wind. The tiny hard granules of snow took a whip to my face and I started tearing immediately. The tears ran down my cheeks from the whipping Mother Nature was giving me for God knew what, but I knew damn well I deserved it. Imagine, a guy like me.

I slipped in the street, almost fell and caught myself. People glanced for a second and judged whether I was drunk or not. In a typhoon, if you fell down, they'd try and figure out if you were drinking or not. People. Where do they really come from? And why are there always more of them briefly around Christmas and New Years? Mysteries.

I walked across the black and white marble entryway outside the bank. It had thin brass banding between the colors of marble to make a mosaic design. It meant that it wasn't really marble, but cast marble. I grabbed the bronze door handle, pulling it against the wind. The giant thick glass door opened and I forced my way in.

Inside it was warm and the smell of perfume and aftershave lotion freshly applied came through. People were beginning to come in behind me. I brushed the snow off as I walked toward the marble walls. Against the walls at regular intervals in the four-story vaulted mezzanine were dark oak wall desks where checks could be made out, funds withdrawn. I removed my gloves and blew into my hands to warm them. I went to a wall desk, shook all of the wetness from my sleeves and jammed my gloves into my coat pocket.

Carefully I opened my sketchpad and set it out before me on the black and green marble top. Mounted into the marble top, all polished and cool, was a bronze cast inkwell with a straight long fountain pen standing straight out of it. Carefully I lifted the pen, saw the thick jet-black ink on its nib. I touched the point to the bronze sheath and let the excess drop find its way back down into the inkwell. I held it gently and moved it over the white paper and began to make my marks.

The rich black ink came out fluidly, brilliant against the pure white. Nowhere, nowhere left in America could you find a straight fountain pen. Everything had been converted over to bright blue ballpoint pens. The river of perfectly controlled black ink came onto my page and made lines for me. It knew how much I loved it. It knew that it was the last of its kind.

I made waveforms like my father, the artist who had taught me. I made continuous infinity signs. I filled a page with repeating round forms and blew on the page until it dried. Inside of me, I felt happy. I had found a thinnest thread that led back in time. I could feel the past as though I were the one elected to come here, to see the marble, to dip the fountain pen, and of a hundred thousand people over centuries of time, to be the one who understood what was ending, to be the one who knew what was just ahead, and to feel for just a few minutes all that was being forgotten in the rush.

When the armed guard at the door repositioned himself to watch me, I understood that it was time to go. It would not be long before this too was converted to a bright blue throwaway ballpoint pen. The guard would watch the blue ballpoint pens just the same. He would guard anything he was told to guard. I closed my notebook and put my gloves back on. Under my arm I carried the last of the sensuality America would tolerate.

•

Summer

Sierra Songs & Descants

Donna Hanelin

Dry Ranges

The point enters the shadow
Dust rises from out of the cracks
Watch the point. It's easy to be happy.
No, dust is not the point
Dust is the remains of the point
The point is a strong young man on a half wild horse
    riding across the high desert
And he's going to find water
He's going to marry a smart sleek woman
His children will glow coral like the western sunset
And his death will take place there —
Just past mid-day on the dry range
Where the point enters the shadow.

Dropped Off in the First Part

Yesterday when I walked home from Viguera
because Berta wasn't there for the intercambio
of English and Spanish and the horse galloped past
down the path with rider and two panting dogs followed
and red ants infested the way so I couldn't stop
to take a photo of oxen eating below in the light
of imminent rainstorm because the ants would sting my feet
if I rested or cover my books if I laid them on the ground
then sting my hands when I picked them up
and since the creek was full I threw my sandals
to the opposite shore and waded across clutching Velazquez
Spanish-English English-Spanish dictionary then slipped
back into my sandals and was headed across the last cornfield
when I saw dark brown thorny branches piled
on the perimeter so had to walk the rutted road past the farm,
listen to the pigs' primeval snorts, scatter the turkeys, suffer
certain odors of the barnyard and return home in the usual way,
up the driveway, and through a green gate; this last part
was all because of the thorns.

Sandra Rockman

True Confessions of a Reluctant Naturalist

1951. First memory. The Bronx. Out in park, pick up crawly thing on grass near foot. "Look, Mommy, how pretty!" Mommy screams. Slaps at hand. Drop bug. Scream. Jump away and cry.

1952. See spider on kitchen floor. Scream for Mommy. Point at spider and cry. Mommy steps on spider. Squooosh. Brown smear on faded yellow linoleum. Ughhh.

1955. Queens. Best friend Franny and I discover an invasion of Japanese beetles on snowball bush in backyard. They look like the glittery gems in Mommy's jewelry box. Pluck 40 of them for jar with holes in the lid. Fight over who keeps it. I win! Place jar on night table. Try to sleep. Think of 40 beetles in the jar, in the bed, in the dark. "Daddy!"

1957. Camp Harmony, Hopewell, NJ. Scheduled time for my bunk's group shower. Open door and see dozens of daddy longlegs in back corner. Refuse to shower until spiders are killed.
   First nature walk. Gary, the counselor, leads us on trail through woods. Finds frog. Does vivisection. Shows us frog heart, frog stomach, frog intestines. After dissection, he turns frog back over and releases it. Frog hops off trail in one bound and stops. I run back to camp and throw up.

1958. Camp Harmony. Refuse to go on nature walks.

1960. Camp Harmony. Boys.

1962-1968. Boys and cigarettes.

1968. Adelphi University, Garden City, Long Island. Urban sociology professor predicts a new population trend of people moving out of cities into rural areas. I think, *He's crazy. Who the hell would want to live in the country?*

1968. Move to Los Angeles.

1969. First camping trip with then-husband and friends to Rosarito Beach, Baja. Successfully smuggle long-haired husband through immigration at Tijuana in secret compartment below false camper floor. Arrive at beach campsite. Mickey and Don are setting up the tents. "Where are the stakes?" asks Mickey. "Steaks," I sing to my growling stomach. (I am not yet the ardent vegetarian I will become.) Don pulls out the tent "stakes." "Oh," I realize with grumbling disappointment. There is a steady sea breeze and Mickey can't get the water to boil but the kids are starving so she pours the pasta into the pot. We eat macaroni and cheese so gluey you could turn the paper plate upside down and nothing would fall to the sand.

1970. First *real* camping trip with then-husband and his friends to Sequoia National Forest near Lake Isabella. The friends are honeymooning, camping their way from New York to California. We set up the tents next to a creek. An extravagant spot, giant trees soothe the harsh Southern California light and heat, the music of running water washes the traffic from my thoughts. Dinner — macaroni and cheese (what else?) at the picnic table. Night falls.

Dark. I am impressed by their collective confidence, sitting and laughing around the campfire. Dark. I am depressed by my discomfort, sitting, not laughing, around the campfire, fretful about sleeping in the open. A tent, after all, is a thin sheet of nylon separating me from a forest and its creatures just waiting to swallow me. As if in response to my thoughts, suddenly from up the drainage, a throaty roar. "What was that?" I whisper, hoping to hide my terror. A flurry of movement. I am the last one in the Toyota.

Dark. A sleepless night dancing the Twist in my borrowed sleeping bag. I am a big beetle in a glass jar.

Light. Next day after lunch, a hike up the narrow trail beside the creek. It is dense with vegetation and soon we are bushwhacking. I can't see forward or back. I can't breathe. Panic attack for neurotic city girl. The forest is swallowing me. "I have to go now . . ." I say and before they can respond, I am crying, sprinting, stumbling back to the campsite where I spend the afternoon alone, in the car, smoking, wishing I were someone else, someone who could breathe in this miraculous place.

1971. The same campsite near Lake Isabella with then-husband and another couple. I have spent the year dreaming about this place, the marbled light, that water music. After lunch, a hike up the narrow trail. Past the spot where I froze last year, the trail resumes and I continue. Up ahead a hundred feet the forest turns orange. The rocks, ground, bushes and tree trunks — orange. It is not the drugs. A billion unspotted ladybugs paint the scenery. It is one of the most amazing sights in my life. I am still breathing.

Farther up the trail the creek widens and pools. We are alone. We strip and go skinny-dipping. First time.

1975. Divorced. Traveling around Europe "to find myself." Carrying backpack. Why is the youth hostel always uphill? In Florence, I run low on money and decide, thriftily, to buy a tent from Ohio gal going home. I begin to brave it in campgrounds just outside cities. I find the countryside in Spain, Portugal, Italy more appealing than the congested cities. In Switzerland, near Luzern, I take a ferry tour on a mountain lake. Across the way I disembark. My eye follows a tiny two-person tram that leads to the top of the mountain. As if in a trance, I get in and ascend alone to a high meadow — misty, green and cool. There are little dots in the distance below me. They are cows. There is a trail and I follow it. I roam for over an hour. Later that evening I realize I have taken a hike. By myself. In the Alps. The photo of me that day was taken on the boat back across the lake. I wear a red nylon jacket. My hair is composed into two braids which descend past my waist. Woven into the braids are yellow and purple wildflowers that I picked on my hike. I am smiling.

1976. Move to Hawaii on Unemployment. Giant cockroaches that fly. Move to San Francisco.

1977. First visit to Grass Valley friend, Barbara. There are handsome men in flannel shirts and tight jeans. They are straight. I think I like it here.

1978. April. Life in San Francisco falls apart. Friend Barbara invites me to move to Grass Valley and live in a finished room in the barn behind her house. Figure I have nothing to lose. First night walk through the backyard to the barn. It is moonless and as dark as I've ever known dark to be. I am more comfortable on Market Street at 3 AM with a purse full of waitressing tips than I am traversing the 60 feet to my room. Stop behind bush to empty bladder. Look up and gasp. I have never seen so many stars. In my room, spider on opposite wall. I tell it, "You stay on your side; I'll stay on mine." Shut off lamp. Sleep.

June. First trip to river at Purdon with Barbara and the kids. River Frank shoots, tries to kill us. We hike downstream instead, take off our clothes and jump into the surge. I look up and down the river canyon, admiring the sculpted elegance of the boulders, the brave pines clinging to the steeps, the shining kids riding the currents. I marvel, *I live here.*

Later that summer, someone at the county fair gives me a button that reads, "I'm rural and I like it." I can hear a taunting voice in my head — "Who the hell would live in the country?"

I live here now. I am smiling. I am breathing.

Doc Dachtler

Tick Removal Cocktail

The most important thing is
DON'T PANIC!
It's just a little tick
burrowing under your skin,
sucking your blood.
Don't go yanking it out.
You'll tear the body away from the head
which will stay attached,
giving you blood poisoning.
Be calm.
Have a drink.
Be a perfect host.
Mix up one for your tick guest as follows:
      5 drops liquid dish soap
      splash of good whiskey
      mix with Q-tip.
Swab the tick gently with this cocktail.
See the little legs kicking.
The tick is getting very drunk and relaxed.
See the little legs stop kicking.
The guest has now O.D.'d. Too bad!
Swab that tick back and forth about twenty times
with generous amounts of cocktail.
The whiskey will carry the soap down around
the head and mouth parts of the tick.
This lubricates the area for easy removal.
Wait about 5 minutes.
Pull the tick out with your fingernails.

P.S. If a rash develops around the bite in a few days or if you feel bad a month or so later for
no apparent reason, get a blood test for Lyme disease. Some ticks carry this miserable
spirochete and it needs early attention. This recipe for taking ticks off kids was given to me
25 years ago by Sally Clark when I taught in a one room schoolhouse in the woods. It has
worked every time. Backpackers can premix the cocktail in a small plastic vial for the trail.

Firewood

for Steve Sanfield

We stacked each other
with armloads of oak
like freshmen with new ideas.

They were light
the first five steps.

Doc Dachtler

Why am I telling you this?

I'm putting a lockset in a downstairs apartment. The owner is the mother of a friend I lost track of 25 years ago. When I find this out I ask her how Dot is doing these days.

"She doesn't speak to me anymore. I was named executrix of the estate when her grandfather died and this made her mad. She stomped out of a room full of lawyers, accountants, and bank people yelling at me, 'You better not screw this up!' and hasn't spoken a single word to me since. I mean, he was my father and I had taken care of him in his last years. It was a complicated estate. It took me over a year to wrap it up, but everyone received their designated share and there was no IRS audit.

"This has been going on, this not speaking, for seven years now. If I could only even just figure it out it would be such a relief. Now there isn't any family to talk to, confide in now and then, like you would with a daughter. As I get into my sixties, well, it becomes more important. Maybe it's because she is a big city, hot-shot lawyer. The worst is, I don't even get to see the grandchildren anymore. I've missed seeing them grow from children to teenagers, to college students. It cuts a piece of your life, your heart, right out.

"Seven long years of it now. Then my husband died so my daughter's the only family I have left. I'm not a bad person or anything. I didn't abuse or neglect my child or any living thing, ever, in my whole life. I don't deserve this, do I?"

I am standing very still with a chisel in one hand, a hammer in the other. I open my eyes wide, shrug up my shoulders.

"I'm sure not!"

She looks at me for a long time. My tongue is lost. She lets out a big sigh, "Why am I telling you this?"

Nate Johnson

Leaving the Garden

I first discovered my family was different at a Lake Vera potluck. Up to that point in my life, a venerable five years long, I had assumed we were perfectly normal. Living in an isolated town in the California foothills with a healthy serving of people who resembled us, I had never questioned our way of life. We had no TV and, though we read, families tend to dissolve into the background in children's literature. Children cannot become heroes if they have parents standing in the way, so authors kill off the adults or separate them from their children or simply dress them in dark floral prints and force them to sit in matching armchairs.

My mother ran a daycare center out of the house, and every day an assorted group of transient adults delivered a throng of companions to my door. With this influx of friends I seldom went over to other houses, and, because my mother and father acted as secondary parents to these children, I assumed that their families were structured like ours.

When we went to the potluck at Lake Vera, I was innocent to any possibility that others might see our way of life as strange. Children ran up and down the lake shore. I was taken aback at their lack of interest in me. At home, on my own turf, my whims led fashion by the nose. I was responsible for massive comebacks in sandbox popularity and for the re-vogueing of the swing set.

At the potluck, the kids were having a great time with each other, but they paid no attention to me. They ran past in screaming waves, playing tag or just racing. Then, following some other, wholly unknown trendsetter, the children dove, ran and tiptoed into the lake.

Lake Vera is a miserable little algae farm, but at five it looked marvelous. A platform floated not far from shore, filled to capacity. Laughter and shouts echoed across the darkening summer evening. It was too much for me. I had to join in.

I pulled at my father's pant leg and told him I wanted to go swimming.

"Okay," he said, "we didn't bring a swimming suit, but you can skinny dip."

This sounded perfectly reasonable to me. Nakedness had always been an integral part of our household. My father believed that it was better to sleep naked, for one thing.

"Gives your balls a chance to breathe," he had told me.

When sleeping naked I certainly wasn't going to bother with clothes each time I went to the bathroom, got a glass of water or even, for that matter, when I wandered out into the dining room for breakfast. If we were hot, we would take off our clothes. It just made sense. If I wanted to go swimming, why get a pair of shorts wet in the process?

I stripped down and made for the water, my pudgy little brother hard at my heels. As we swam toward the platform my excitement mounted. They were playing king of the hill, pushing at each other, forming alliances, betraying them, and splashing into the water in glorious defeat. I reached the little raft and pulled my body up, bracing myself to take all comers. Instead of rushing me, everyone stopped.

My brother was struggling on board when a treble voice shrieked, "They're naked! They're naked!" and all the boys and girls dove off the other side. The platform was completely empty, save my brother and me. I tried to savor having this little kingdom to myself. I half-heartedly pushed my brother off the platform a few times, but there was no satisfaction in it.

Demoralized, we swam back to shore and put our clothes on. I felt an odd sort of shyness the rest of the evening and stayed close behind my mother's legs.

Never before had I been ostracized for public nudity. During the summer my family would drive the narrow, twisting road to the old green bridge, then hike down the steep gorge of the Yuba River. Often we would have a little beach to ourselves, but on weekends the rocks and sand would be covered with families. Dogs swam back and forth, barked at each other and raced along the shore. Bags of miniature soy-flavored rice cakes were opened and shared. Babies in sun hats tottered about or sat in the shallows eating sand. Teenagers dove off rocks to catch Frisbees in the air. Nobody ever wore anything more than a thin layer of SPF 30.

I studied the girls. Unlike my mom, they had no hair between their legs and it was easy to see how different we were. What did it feel like to have that slim fold instead of the rubbery, bouncing penis? Where did the pee come out?

Everywhere there were different bodies: Huge bodies and tiny ones, smooth and hairy, hips that jutted or swelled or did not even interrupt the flow from leg to waist, breasts that covered entire chests or sat respectfully apart, stomachs that bulged or rippled or sagged, penises circumcised or foreskinned, dangling or contracted.

At times this variation fascinated me and I would watch the people attentively. It was interesting to see an unusual body, a terrifically fat man, for example, without the obscuring clothes. I stared at these people fixedly, and when they looked back at me, I would simply smile and, more often than not, they would smile back.

Most of the time, however, my attention was devoted to building sand castles and exploring upstream. Coming home from the river, my brother and I would doze in the back seat heat of the old station wagon while my father listened to the Giants game through the static of the AM radio.

The fall after the potluck, when I ventured out of my home to enter first grade, I would grow quiet when older kids spoke derisively about all the weirdos at the Yuba. I became painfully aware of my family's differences, our faults, I thought at the time. From that first evening at Lake Vera I began to suspect we lacked some vital widget in the family engine. As I grew older this feeling condensed into a puddle of resentment. Why weren't my parents normal? I wondered angrily. Still, I loved the idea of us together, the feeling I got when my parents read outloud each night, or when the first autumn storm bent the pines and we made hot chocolate, or when I sang with Mother and her guitar.

When I began to learn how the world worked, how backward and primitive we were, I was mortified. I remember perhaps a year after the potluck a babysitter commenting on the family.

"You guys live like animals," she said.

I couldn't speak to her. I went outside, closed the door and sat on the deck, my back against the wall and my arms crossed. I wouldn't have been offended if I was not so sure it was true. I had, by this time, seen other houses very different from our own, houses on whose shining white carpets sat pastel furniture and glass coffee tables on which magazines were arranged in perfect fans. These families went to church on Sundays, the girls took ballet, the boys were star pitchers, and *nobody* was ever naked. I was greatly concerned, for obviously I had been born into a family lacking the moral fiber necessary to keep a house white and spotless. I had become soft under the constant shower of loving affirmations, an integral part of my rearing. Since my parents never rapped my knuckles when I ate with my fingers, allowed me to go naked and abstain from church, I would never be a star pitcher, or a cheerleader's boyfriend or any sort of clean, crew-cut hero like the boys in the books.

In reflection, I realize that my life was in some ways harder than those of the children in the families I admired. My parents absolutely forbade the customary childhood vices. We were not allowed to watch movies or television, even at friends' houses. Neither my brother nor I was allowed to have refined sugar or chocolate except on very special occasions like Christmas. For dessert we might have rice pudding, sweetened with raisins. When my brother came down with milk and wheat allergies, these too were eliminated from our diet. Brown rice, string beans, corn tortillas and soy milk figured large in my early life.

As the children, we were expected to do our share of the house-work. Every Sunday morning we divided up the jobs and turned the house upside down. I didn't know that in the gleaming white families, the mother was usually responsible for all the cleaning, while the children practiced their *pliés* and curve balls. Though we were not immaculate, my family most certainly did not live like animals. I was shocked when I visited the babysitter several years later and found that she did not have a perfect house but a somewhat shabby home covered in a liberal sprinkling of cat hair.

Apart from Sunday clean-up, my brother and I helped with the cooking and washing. When winter came we stacked cords of oak and cedar. My parents never consented to buy a television, but they did buy a little IBM with an amber monochrome screen. Mom made it very clear that the computer was for my father's writing, not for games. Soon enough, though, Dad's curiosity got the better of him and we installed "Space Quest." Our playtime, however, was strictly regulated. We could play for half an hour on the computer only after we had spent three hours outside. I went to great lengths to fill those three hours every day. I remember my brother and I sitting, huddled together on the covered deck in mid-winter. We had ensconced ourselves in layers of blankets and took turns holding a little digital clock. Beyond the shelter of the roof, sleet spattered against the ground. The chimes clanged wildly in the wind.

"How close are we getting to the first hour?" I would ask.

My brother would look down at the clock. "It's been eleven minutes."

Other days, when the weather was better or when there was enough snow to go sledding, the requisite three hours came easily. My mother is fond of telling me I once said, "This way we win twice. We get to have fun outside *and* play the computer." I suspect I made this saccharine remark to curry favor, in hope of a more lenient system for, though what I said was technically true, I never liked it when my half hour was up. I was madly envious of my friends who played "Legend of Zelda" on their Nintendo to their hearts' content.

Sierra Songs & Descants

As I grew older and spent less and less time at home, my sense of being an outsider increased. It seemed there was some sort of secret society which existed beyond my realm of knowledge. How else could one explain the way the elite echelon of boys and girls knew each other even before the first day of classes? How else could they all know what clothes to wear, what jokes to tell and what music to like?

What seemed some great unifying secret was probably no more than the manifestation of my feeling out of place, like so many other teens. The sudden exposure to pop culture added momentarily to my bewilderment. I fell in love with the forbidden fruits of my childhood. But, though the breadth of American pop was overwhelming, I found its depth illusory, and I emerged on the other side, ambivalent. Much media is crap, I decided. Still, I was in love with the play of light, sound and information across the screen. I was in love with the mean, edgy humor of Hollywood and New York, which so well relieved the kind but meaningless affirmations of my parents. I was in love, yet I felt I was immune. I had passed beyond the curtain and I could see, I thought, the wildebeest herd of the normal, thundering through the desert in the zigzag chase of who knows what shimmering reproduction of a fairy tale. After all, I was different.

A few years ago, I went back to the old bridge over the Yuba with my brother, both of us visiting from the outside world. Fall had brought a chill to the river and chased out the bathers. The low sun bronzed the water and deepened the chipped green finish of the bridge. A battered black truck coughed its way down the hill and clattered the timbers of the driving surface. We moved out of the way, up against the railing. The truck stopped and a wrinkled woman with wild hair stuck her head out of the window.

"Great, isn't it? I like to just come down here and sit sometimes. It makes you feel better when you do that, the ions get you. Lot of ions 'round here. Negative ions, negative but they're positive. I mean you want the negative ions. Positive equals negative. You know what I mean. But the river's great, huh? It's just, whew!" She made a sort of sweeping *Heil Hitler* motion out the window, down the river and toward the sun. "Well, enjoy," and she rattled up the hill leaving a few explosions of exhaust and a cloud of dust.

We looked at each other and we laughed the derisive, self-satisfied laugh reserved for those who know better. Then, with genuine affection, he said, "I love this place."

I just smiled.

Will Baker

Balance

I found the rattler in a net slung
over grapevines to keep out birds,
woven square by square tight
and tighter, until he could do nothing
but announce himself, like seeds in a gourd.

His jaw was forced ajar, little fangs
delicate as kitten claws. Mica eyes.
The long bagged muscle of him
oozing back and forth for days
in this cloud of dark lace, waiting for me.

I thought of his like who had crossed me free:
coiled and buzzed and flung away, vanished
in a breath, an angel's whip, or beheaded
with hoe or scythe, or stuck in a peach basket
to show the kids. The one around my hat,
another fried in butter for a lark.

With scissors, strand by strand, I cut him loose.
The head was not easy: his will one way
only, yet always angling. A last knot
snipped and he dropped like a stretch of taffy.

He tried to arrow off, but his backbone
kinked. He was skew, an invalid. A jerky
lunge, a hitch-hitch, was all he could. No zero
at my bone. Rather pity for this old Satan,
this lame, anxious hero in a hurry.

My thoughts snarled and ran, a new-hatched brood —
the way I sleep and rise and bend and eat —
strip hides, crack bones, scrape scales, drag out guts —
a large, careless beast and his rank debris —
this world a slaughter-pen where old men snore
in their bloody boots, the auction ended.

Better to lengthen, quiet in the soft dust,
then quicken into one stroke of light,
swallow the afternoon and pleat oneself
back into the shadows, the earth. Assume
no final shape. Wait only for release.
Balance between motion and rest, beyond
hope. Sing in your prison. Rattle the gourd.

Oakley Hall

Excerpt from
Ambrose Bierce and the One-Eyed Jacks,
Chapter Two

SUCCESS, n. *The one unpardonable sin against one's fellows.*
— *The Devil's Dictionary*

SUNDAY, MAY 2, 1891

I had encountered Miss Winifred Sweet, the *Examiner's* Annie
Laurie, in the hallways at the newspaper but had never met her
formally until a picnic arranged by Willie Hearst on Angel Island the
Sunday after my encounter with Miss Lindley. Boarding Willie's steam
launch *Aquila*, with a hand from Ah Sook, Willie's Chinese boy, at the
Jackson Street wharf were Miss Sweet, Bierce, Sam Chamberlain and
me. Miss Powers, Willie Hearst, and another lady were already aboard.
It was my first sight of Willie's mistress, whom he kept in a mansion
called Sea Point in Sausalito, across the Bay from the City, from where
he commuted to the *Examiner* on the *Aquila*. His situation with Miss
Powers, and the massive fact of his mother's disapproval of it, were the
talk of the *Examiner* staff. He made no effort to keep his liaison a
secret, displaying Miss Tessie Powers proudly and publicly. She was a
very pretty lady with a shy smile, a face framed with curls and a kind of
serenity draped around her like a shawl.

I was surprised to see that the other woman already aboard was Miss
Lindley, her near-sighted face peering unsmiling at me from beneath a
black straw bonnet. She wore a tartan cloak over her shoulders.

Will Hearst was reputed to mount these parties and picnics for
selected members of the *Examiner's* staff for purposes of understanding
and cooperation, but seeing Miss Lindley I understood that she and I
had been included in this rather august company because of the latest
piece that I had submitted to Sam Chamberlain.

When we chuffed away from the dock, with Ah Sook passing
glasses of champagne from galvanized tubs brimming with ice and
champagne bottles, Will Hearst stood stiff-backed and nautical-capped

at the wheel. He was 28 years old, but he looked much younger, tall and slender, with a pink and white complexion and a little golden moustache. He was usually slightly diffident in manner except, I observed, aboard the *Aquila*, where he was very much the commander.

He had a high-pitched voice that had refused to grow up with him. He was a good listener. He gave the speaker his full attention, eyeing him with that unwavering bug-eyed gaze that some found unnerving. His answers were formal, he addressed everyone as "Mister," he would not allow anyone to follow him through a door.

With dramatic spinnings of the wheel, Willie maneuvered the *Aquila* through the massed hulls of old sailing ships beneath a thicket of masts and spars into the open Bay, the eastern foothills rising to the right, the camel hump of Angel Island straight ahead, scows under tow to the left, with a high scarf of smoke from the tugboat.

On the noisy passage to Angel Island we were seated in parallel rows on upholstered benches beneath a gleaming-varnished canopy, gazing at each other behind Will Hearst's back. I was seated next to Miss Lindley, Sam Chamberlain beside Miss Powers, but these two ladies were acquainted with each other from back East and frequently chatted across the aisle. Bierce, whom I knew to be cynical about this kind of outing, stood gazing back at the City with his hands clasped behind his back.

Miss Sweet, red-haired and green-eyed, in her crisp cotton blouse and long skirt, had risen from her seat, and rather (I thought) paraded herself, striding up and down with a light step, uttering cries of appreciation at the fancy fittings and upholstery of the *Aquila*. Winnie Sweet had come to the *Examiner* from playing in a traveling theater company of *The Two Orphans*, in which she had impressed Sam Chamberlain.

Miss Powers wore a fluttery blue dress and made some efforts to direct Ah Sook in the passing of the champagne glasses. It was clear that the Chinaman loved his mistress. It was well-known that Willie Hearst had collected Miss Powers when he was a student at Harvard. He had brought her west to San Francisco when he had taken over at the *Examiner*, where the fact of her existence drove his mother to distraction.

Feet braced against the motion of the *Aquila*, Miss Sweet complained of the difficulties of writing text for the approval of Mr. Hearst and Mr. Chamberlain.

"Mr. Bierce will no doubt be pleased to instruct you in proper journalistic usage," Willie advised her, turning from his stance at the wheel, his long legs in white flannel trousers spread, hands gripping the gleaming spokes.

I thought that Bierce, who was easy to offend, might be sensitive to this, but apparently he too was impressed by Miss Sweet. Watching him, I thought I would never understand this strange person. Miss Sweet had turned to face him.

"First the necessity of concentrating on the specific rather than the general, my dear," Bierce said.

Miss Sweet's expression as she leaned toward him was all ears.

"Local man appointed to post," he said. "That is a phrase distinguished by its total lack of information. May I also cite 'a pluvial dispensation,' a term I was disappointed to come across in Monday's *Examiner*."

He grinned at Willie's back.

"'Rain' is better, you see," he continued, "as it is not pompous and inflated diction. 'Drops battered the leaves of the petunias,' is more effective still. It is visual and aural. There is nothing visual about a 'pluvial dispensation.' Journalism seeks to show, not to impress with the journalist's vocabulary."

"This is very interesting, Mr. Bierce!" Miss Sweet's fidgeting had quieted like a patted colt under Bierce's steady regard.

Miss Powers sat watching him from her own quietness. Miss Lindley had put down her untasted champagne glass on a little varnished shelf, where it jiggled hazardously until she took it up again.

"You perhaps noticed the verb 'battered' in my previous quotation," Bierce went on. "Battered is a strong verb. Strong verbs are more effective than weak verbs bolstered by adverbs. You are cognizant with the parts of speech, Miss Sweet?"

"I am sir. I was well-schooled in Wisconsin."

"'Battered,' you understand, is more effective than 'violently activated,' or 'knocked about wildly.'"

"Yes, I do see!"

"There is a feminine style," Bierce said. "It employs a large dosage of adverbs and adjectives. It is called 'feminine overemphatic.' There is also the feminine fallacy of over-modification. A masculine sentence will usually end with the exclamation mark — (if there is to be one) — at the end of the sentence. A feminine sentence would have the exclamation mark somewhere in the middle followed by one or two modifying phrases or clauses, if you catch my meaning."

"But, Mr. Bierce, would it not be proper for a feminine journalist to employ a more feminine style than a masculine one, with all those exclamation marks at the end of the sentences?"

Sam Chamberlain let out a whoop of a laugh, and I saw from the stricture of Willie Hearst's nostrils as he turned to glance back at us that he was blocking his own laughter. Miss Powers looked sweetly puzzled. Miss Lindley raised her eyebrows at me. Bierce proffered his glass to Ah Sook for a refill.

"That may be true, Miss Sweet, but the female journalist must not let her nouns and verbs be swamped amongst the multitudinous seas of adverbs and adjectives of the female novelists, such as Mrs. Gertrude Atherton."

That seemed to me to have answered Winnie Sweet's pertness.

"And remember," Bierce said. "Only a genius can afford to employ more than one adjective per noun. And that, my dear, only the very choicest."

"Ah, well, Mr. Bierce," Miss Sweet said, straightening and smiling around at the rest of her auditors, "at the *Examiner* I am surrounded by geniuses on every hand — the most outrageous, incredible, ridiculous, glorious set of geniuses one has ever encountered!

"Now, how are those adjectives, Mr. Bierce?"

"Quite perfectly redundant, sentimental and feminine, Miss Sweet. And charming."

Now everyone was laughing, and Miss Sweet had carried the day. "One perseveres, Mr. Bierce!"

"Perseverance is usually counted a virtue, Miss Sweet. Except in the case of female poets."

More laughter, as Bierce gained the upper hand again.

"Oh, I am not a poet, Mr. Bierce," Miss Sweet said.

"I am well aware of that, Miss Sweet," Bierce said with a bow.

Daniel Williams

Live Tornado

Down south near Copper
They had this place
They called 'Coyote Alley'

It was just some barbed wire
Ran up and down
Over the hillsides

The ranchers shot coyotes
From their trucks — hauled
Them down there

Hung them by their tails
Males females pups
Sixty to a hundred at a time

When the wind was right
You could tell
You were near Copperopolis

The air above you black
And thick with vultures

A live tornado

Tree Topper

When you're up there seventy feet or so
All that's between you
And a hot slivery slide
Down hell's banister
Are spikes and a leather belt

It's mighty lonesome
After you've cut your notch
Got your hinge
And there's only 2 inches of wood
Between you and what happens next

And what happens next
Can be mighty various

Maybe twenty feet
Of heavy wet tree above your head
Can hinge back
Hammer you in the goddamnedest nutcracker
Make you one dimensional real fast

Or maybe that mast leans over
Where you want it

But you've weakened what's left standing
Or piss-ants have chewed its insides
Causing a split to ride down its trunk
And both halves scissor
Catching you in the pinch

They carry you out two pieces in one bag

But most times the sonuvabitch goes where you want it
And there you are
Swinging like a damn monkey on a stick
Grinning to beat hell in sudden sunshine

Molly Giles

Sloane's Girl

Until the day of the faculty farewell, Mavis Trout was a beautiful woman. Even that day, mid-May of her 65th year, heads turned as she strode out of the auditorium and crossed the campus to the Composition Center. Her silver hair swung in a sleek pageboy and her hips swiveled like a girl's. With the help of two plastic surgeons, both of whom had propositioned her, she had retained the crazed kitten's face she'd been born with: small, sharply boned and freckled, with a bip of a nose and round, slightly crossed blue eyes that popped with intelligence and hostility. Her waist had thickened, her voice had thinned, and her mind had started to wander, but her mind had always wandered, that was its job, that was what made her such a good teacher. Who wanted a mind that stayed at home? Who wanted anything that stayed at home?

"Not I," said Mavis Trout, stalking up the stairs to her office. She ignored the girl waiting outside in the hall, plunged her key into the lock, kicked the door open, sank into the revolving chair behind her desk and turned toward the window, exposing a length of milky crinkled thigh beneath her slit black skirt.

The girl, Jenny Sanchez, hesitated. She had been to the farewell and had seen Dr. Trout drop the plaque at the dean's feet. But her paper was finished, and it was late, and she needed it to get a grade. She took a deep breath, hunched her backpack off her shoulders and entered.

"Welcome," Mavis said without turning around. "You have the great honor of being the last student I will ever see."

Jenny eased her backpack onto the weird fur couch Dr. Trout kept in the corner and unzipped it to look for her paper. "Thank you," she said. She shuffled through folders and textbooks, panicked. Where was her paper? What if she'd forgotten it this morning in her rush to get out of the apartment? What if it was still on the kitchen table? Or on the bus?

"Forced retirement," Mavis continued. "What a concept. Perfectly legal. Perfectly evil. Goodbye. Goodluck. And now get the hell out of here."

Jenny looked up, but Dr. Trout was not talking to her and when she looked down she saw her paper. It was stained where she'd spilled her coffee and wrinkled where the baby had grabbed it. She'd had trouble with the printer at the computer lab and some of the sentences were spaced on a slant. She smoothed the paper flat between both hands, the way her grandmother patted out tortillas. She was worried because Dr. Trout often gave students grades she'd made up: M for Messy or IBS for Illiterate Bull Shit. You had to petition Administration to get those grades changed before you could pass.

"So now what?" Mavis asked. "What should I do now with the rest of my life?"

Jenny shook her head, relieved, and offered the paper.

"I'm talking to you, dear. What should I do?"

Jenny dropped her eyes. Her paper was titled ESSAY NUMBER FOUR. The assignment had been to write an oral history from people you knew. She had interviewed Emilio and two of his brothers about being laid off at the garage. "Spend time with your family?" she suggested. Her voice came out squeaky. It was not the low calm voice she planned to use when she graduated and found work as a drug and alcohol counselor. "You will have time to be with your family," she said more firmly.

"I have no family."

"You have a husband," Jenny said, confused. "I saw him at the faculty farewell."

"Oh," Mavis slid her silver bracelets up and down her thin arms. "Sloane."

"The writer."

"The literary biographer," Mavis corrected her. "The gossip. The spy. The ancient betrayer."

Jenny frowned, uncertain. The old man had sat erect, staring eagerly at Dr. Trout throughout the ceremony as if he were a deaf mute and she were his signer. Maybe he really was a deaf mute. One of Jenny's sister's boys had been born that way. But no, Dr. Trout had been the silent one. She had sat on the podium like a queen, her eyes the exact blue of the ribbon the dean had draped over her neck and she had not said a word, not even when she dropped the plaque and walked out. Only the old man had broken the silence. "Isn't she wonderful?" he had cried, to no one, his voice high as a bird's. "Isn't she marvelous?"

"It looked like he loved you a lot," Jenny said boldly.

"How would you like to be stuck with someone who 'loved you a lot'?" Mavis asked. "Day in and day out."

Jenny, thinking of the baby left at daycare, shrugged and fixed her eyes on the photographs on the wall. They showed Dr. Trout in a low cut black dress standing with a series of strange looking men: a short curly headed man in sunglasses, a tall hunch-shouldered man in a tweed jacket, a fat dark eyed boy in fur. The men looked the same in every picture, proud and wet-lipped, and Dr. Trout looked the same, too, sort of sexy and mad as hell. Jenny shivered.

Mavis followed her eyes. "Poet. Novelist. Playwright. Sloane's famous subjects. Of course half of them are dead now. Most of them were dead before. This one," she tapped the man in the sunglasses, "couldn't keep it up and this one never came. Sloane loved hearing things like that. Of course Sloane has been impotent for years. Thank God."

Jenny nodded and held her paper out.

"So without this career," Mavis said, "if that's what it is, if teaching composition to incompetents for thirty years can be called a career, I am without resource. There is nothing else I can do. All I've ever known is the difference between *lie* and *lay* and *lying* and *getting laid*." She laughed, then her voice rose. "So you see my predicament. I'll be forced to look at Sloane, listen to Sloane, live with Sloane. Which is exactly what he's always wanted. Last night he said, and he didn't even care when I screamed, 'This is going to be like a second honeymoon.' Christ. Wasn't the first one bad enough? Do you know how long we've been married?"

Jenny opened her mouth, closed it.

"Forty-two years," Mavis said. "Do you know why we got married? Because I thought he could help me. Do you know why we stayed married? Because he could not. You of course do not understand that."

"No," Jenny agreed.

"Nor should you have to. It goes beyond the complexities of Comp 102."

Jenny nodded and glanced at her wristwatch. She had to catch the bus, get the baby, and meet Emilio at the courthouse in an hour. She looked up, startled to see Dr. Trout's popped eyes fixed on her navel. She reached to tug her tee shirt down.

"Where did you get that tattoo," Mavis asked. "What is it? A spider?"

"Sunflower," Jenny said.

"Well, give me your stupid little paper." Mavis took it, scrawled a huge A on top and handed it back.

"You're not even going to read it?"

"You were the only student who came to the faculty farewell," Mavis explained.

"I thought we had to."

"You did? Well. That was a waste of your day, wasn't it? Tell me," Mavis swiveled away toward the window again. "Have I taught you anything?"

"No," Jenny said, furious.

Mavis laughed. "I didn't think so. Well. Goodbye, dear. Good luck. Now get out."

Jenny grabbed her backpack and slammed out the door. Mavis heard her army boots drum down the hallway. Then, feeling like an actress, the way she had felt all her life in fact, she began to pack her books as she imagined an actress playing a professor packing her books for the last time would pack them. Showily, one by one, she picked up Sloane's biographies, put on her reading glasses, and read the titles out loud in a mocking singsong: MIDDLE YEARS OF A MIDDLE-WEIGHT, NAKED NARCISSUS, FIRST PERSON SINGULAR. She did not need to open the books to read the dedications: "To My Girl, Without Whom" etcetera. *Pimp*, she thought, as she'd always thought, the word plump and easy in her mind.

She turned and walked to the window. She could jump. She could throw the chair, the photos, and all the books out. But what good would that do. They were all replaceable. She herself was replaceable. No, she'd do what she'd meant to do. She'd give F's to everyone but the Sanchez girl and then she'd do what she'd never thought of before: she'd go to a tattoo parlor and get herself covered in spiders and come home and walk into Sloane's bedroom as recklessly and wearily as she'd ever walked into the rooms of the others he'd sent her to, and she'd take off her clothes and pivot naked in front of him until he wept. Then she'd pack her suitcase and leave. It was time to retire.

Steve Sanfield

Sierra Song

those honking geese
draw me outside
for the rising sun

on this bright summer morning
stream and hummingbird
are my breakfast music

seen in the flight
of the red tail hawk
the distant hills

true eloquence
the rattlesnake's
warning

my nap
would have been longer
but for the buzzing fly

mosquitoes
boldly announcing
their plans

an eagle soars
I watch
only its shadow

like my grandmother's lullaby
the wind
in the pines

everyone asleep
except me
and that owl

Judy Brackett Crowe

Lilies

Only four of the old nuns are left, retired Sisters of Mercy, come here
to live out their last days on the third floor of the old convent above
the school. Former teachers, all of them, from Dakota, Nebraska, Iowa.
Only Sister Mary Sophie, ninety-something, ventures down the stairs
to the school or the grounds or the chapel anymore — invisible, or so
she likes to think, tiptoeing through the halls in black sturdy shoes.
Her habit, once black wool head to toe, is navy blue, — shirt, sweater,
skirt, stockings. Covering her short white hair, a wimple still, though
they told her years ago she didn't have to wear that anymore either.

The rosary she made as a girl travels in her sweater pocket, and she
fingers the beads constantly. Strung and restrung dozens of times, kernels
of dried corn and grapefruit seeds, the cross her brother Seth — or was it
Teddy? — carved from the hard wood of the Osage orange, that thorny
tree, miles and miles of them along the lane between her family's farm and
the next one. Her brother told her Plains Indians had used the same strong
wood for bows.

Sometimes, amidst the murmurs, the giggles, the teachers' voices
spilling out the classroom doors, the smells of chalk and children, she
thinks she sees herself, the thin lank-haired girl she used to be, slip
around the corner just ahead. She slows or stops a moment. What
would she do if she caught up to herself, plain girl, Plains girl? What
would she say? What might that girl say back?

Nights, too, middles-of-the-nights, Sister Mary Sophie haunts the
halls and classrooms. When there's a good moon, it's bright as day, and
so comfortable to be there, inside the kind of space and smells where
she spent so many years. It's as if the children's things belong to her —
books and pencils, red sweaters and jump ropes hanging on the hooks
in back, a box in the corner filled with scarred baseballs and big rubber
balls for four-square. She sits at a table in a child-size chair and looks
around and looks back.

She likes the grounds around the chapel, too — St. Joseph
standing watch; the fountain; the ancient, lush though unkempt trees,

hedges, and shrubs a tranquil hodgepodge, grown from seeds and slips brought in from everywhere, like the people here, like Sister Mary Sophie. Many of the trees must be as old as she or even older — an English yew, a Norway spruce, a glorious sugar maple whose leaves will soon catch fire. Algerian ivy and other creepers climb the walls and trees, their fingers slipping under clapboards on the chapel walls.

Daytimes, the students and the garden clubbers come, straw hats and notebooks and cameras, to walk the paths, pointing here and there, rubbing leaves between their fingers. She listens to these garden fans, who call the greenery by formal names as if they're not yet on a first-name basis — *Taxus baccata, Buxus sempervirens 'Suffruticosa,' Acer saccharum.* They sound like prayers, and Sister Mary Sophie has learned them all.

She's the fondest of the lily, *Amaryllis belladonna*, Naked Lady, Beautiful Woman, that lives at the bottom of the stairs. At first, she blushed even to think the name. Throughout the year, it has all beauty and plainness and impassivity, but only one of those at a time. The huge old bulb, multiplying itself for decades, lumpy in the dirt, just sits until summer, then sends up brown stalks, slender as girls, about the height of the first-graders, with fragrant trumpet flowers the rose-pink of Nebraska hollyhocks, clusters of six, eight, ten, that last for weeks. In fall and winter, after the blooms curl, dry, and die away, bold leafspears rise.

God's grandeur in this place is vertical — the pointy-needled tops of pines and firs poke the heavens, but there seems less of heaven here than where Sister Mary Sophie came from. On those plains and rolling hills, the stars and heavens settle down around you. She feels a stranger in this strange land. And there's not a cottonwood in sight. She'd give an orange, a juicy California lunchbox orange, to hear the rattle of the cottonwoods in fall just one more time.

Tonight, one of those sleepless half-moon nights, she roams through the empty classrooms. First grade. Sister Mary Michael Ann. The board next to the teacher's desk is covered with purple felt, and a golden halo encircles Jesus' face. Photos of the first-grade children with their missing teeth and guileless smiles are spread around Him, always one or two outside the circle. Those misbehavers have been moved "away from Jesus." Sister Mary Sophie often hears the teachers scolding them.

The dark-haired boy with earnest eyes is outside, down in the corner, again. Sister Mary Sophie clucks her tongue, looks over her shoulder, and puts him back up with the rest. She pats the photo as if to smooth his hair. Jesus would not stand for such a thing. Looking at this dark-haired boy, she remembers: Teddy was the one who put night crawlers on her fishhooks. It *was* Seth who carved the cross.

She knows the sad and happy truth is that everything falls away — family, friends, even the fervor she once felt for all of this. She prays, of course, still prays without ceasing, but her prayers are higher now and lighter, a kind of hum.

She moves about, straightens the desks, watches the goldfish swimming, eerie in the moonlit tank, pinches dead leaves from the Creeping Charlie, and wanders out and down the hall to the fifth grade room, Mr. Somebody's room, a lay teacher — they're nearly all lay teachers nowadays.

She notes the familiar cursive alphabet card around the room above the blackboard and says the alphabet aloud. She reads the spelling words: DIARY DAIRY DUTIFUL (Yes, it's D week; last week was C — she remembers CANINE and CURIOUS) DIMPLE DRIFT DIVINE. Picking up a stub of chalk she writes in her most careful penmanship: DALMATION. She smiles to herself and walks out to the side door that's never locked and down more stairs to stroll the paths of the garden maze. She absently counts the beads and murmurs: *Ligustrum lucidum, Cedrus deodara, Ilex aquifolium.*

The garden glows in the half-moon's light; the air, Indian summer warm, and the smells of fall, green-turning-gold, at last make her sleepy. She pauses at the Naked Lady, the Beautiful Woman, *Amaryllis belladonna,* thinks all its names, and bends to inhale its rich wet smell. She sighs and says "Amen" and wends her way back to go up to her little bed. As she rounds the corner at the top of the third-floor stairs, her reflection in the rippled window greets her. Looking back at her is that plain girl she was, ninety years ago. She smells the pink smell still, nods to the girl in the glass, and whispers: *Sophia belladonna.* She feels petal-like herself, light enough to float away.

Carlos Reyes

Piute

— for Rich B.

He has been to Rush Creek
near Mono Lake

gathering the old food
in the traditional way

for the old people
the *Ku-za-de-ka:*

the larvae eaters.

He shows me: *Ku-za-vi,*
fly larvae skimmed
from the lake
(grainy, chewy, with
resiny aftertaste)

Piaghi, dried moth caterpillars
captured from the Jeffrey pines

Tu-ba-a, piñon nuts
ground into meal
in a *metate.*

He says, "You try it
sometime."

The next day I find a note:
"*tu-ca,* to eat; i.e. eat"
(to encourage me).

That evening
more instructions:

"Before you eat it, say something
good, like a little prayer.

Say, 'This *ku-za-vi* will be good for me.
Something good will happen
if I eat this piaghi, etc.'"

I hesitate.

He pauses, laughs
his own full laugh
then says:

"You can say it in English."

Kathryn Napier Stull

Leaving the Fair

In the red carnival glow
of ring toss and Ferris wheel,
me and cousin Sarah walk a breeze of relief
along the chain link
full of funnel cake and Coke.
It's the first year I get to wind through
the maze of catcalls and buzzers and spun sugar air
without supervision.

A little blond boy catches my eye
as he stands between two parked cars
leaning in and pulling back
as he waits for the lanes to clear.
I think to myself, in my ten-year-old wisdom,
someone should hold his hand.

He darts out into the slick black street
and a huge gleaming pickup
screaming down the lane
with gnashing silver grill
slaps his small body down to the asphalt.
He pops up like a jumping bean
not realizing that his bones are broken,
then crumples like a dress
slipping from its hanger.

The driver carries him to the gutter
and lays him out,
his stricken eyes
pleading with mine.

I rush over
and Sarah goes for 911
as the driver backs away like a coyote.
I push my jacket beneath his head,
hold his cold hand
and begin telling gentle lies.

He holds my gaze,
eyes shining with fear
amid the flickering disco of crimson light
and the red ink of bloodstreams
coursing from his hair.

He is eight,
his name is Kenny Keasley.
He wants his grandmother.

I tell him his grandmother is coming, is coming.
I tell him I'm not leaving him.
I ask him if he's hurting. He isn't.

The games and rides behind me
become the clank and shift of heavy machinery
from deep underground.
Instead of corndog grease and grape syrup
I smell rubber
and the peat moss aroma of his bloody brow.

He shivers like a sheet of cellophane
and I lean in close,
trying to enfold him in the heat of my love.
He keeps asking for his grandmother
and I keep lying
and squeezing his hand.

It's been too long.
where's Sarah?
where's Grandma?
where's the swift white hand
of emergency?

In the middle of my murmuring,
his eyes fill suddenly with a dark question,
I feel his fingers clasp to mine,
and then his pale hand grows soft.

I am numb as twirling ambulance lights
strobe the ruby night into a frenzy.
I cannot loosen my grip on his fingers.
Someone should hold his hand.
Anonymous arms pull me away.
There is only his face,
white as a tooth,
receding from mine.

You are eight.
Your name is Kenny Keasley.
Your grandmother is coming.

Kathryn Napier Stull

A Clamor of Arachnids

A rustling of silks
embalming life beyond the bed:
the queen mother wraps her prey
with a butcher's fast and practiced hand
and gets fat
while a hundred thousand children
in a pouch near the crown of the net
wait to sprinkle themselves
like milkweed
on the drapes.

Magdalena in the Doorway

Magdalena in the woods, sleeping. Magdalena at the gate, laughing. Magdalena in the bath. One huge eye, Magdalena's, staring with characteristic fury. The canvases are propped at various heights before him. Reginald backs up until his heel hits the far wall of the studio and leans there, defeated. The late afternoon is thick with heat. There's nothing to be done. He takes the thin path to the house, unbuttoning his blue shirt, letting it fly behind him in the breeze.

Magdalena is talking to a friend on the phone. She cackles and throws back her mane of black hair, but when she hears Reginald clink the glasses in the kitchen cabinet for his wine, she lowers her voice and hangs up. She appears at the doorway between the sunroom and the kitchen and watches him drink a full glass standing up, then pour another and walk to the table with the bottle, where he sits, all without looking at her. She sweeps into the dining nook and stands above him, spreads both hands face down on the table very close to his glass, his arm. He doesn't look up.

"Shall we get drunk?" she says in her throaty sharp voice, never any softness, any indecision. She has taught him to speak this way, too. He finally lifts his head — she won't sit; he cranes back to meet her eyes. He looks for something in them, a smile perhaps, danger, pity. There are no secrets in her irises. She is flesh and hair and alarming beauty and open, obvious cruelty. He rises, gets another goblet, sits back down, and pours her a full glass. He pushes it across to her slowly, then raises his cup.

"To beauty."

"To heartbreak."

It is the old toast, the incantation against falling in love, or failing in it, they used to use when they were new, traveling the world and never stopping long enough to feel the heavy breath of boredom wrap its sinews about them. It takes on a different significance now, and Magdalena casts her eyes down briefly, but this time Reginald keeps watch. She has bled him of his shyness, but he's glad to see that some has taken root in her. She tips her glass back and takes half in the first gulp.

"Music!" she declares, and whirls, and is gone.

*

They have been living in the big ranch house for three years now. Reginald built the studio with his friend Roberto in the first year while Magdalena started a garden. It was supposed to supply them with tomatoes and scallions and peppers, but Magdalena couldn't commit to the regimen of watering and weeding and tilling, so dug the whole thing up and cast wildflower seeds heavily across the yard. They grow in a thicket of red and orange and yellow and pink in summer, blue in spring. Reginald and Magdalena sit together sometimes on the bench behind the house and watch the sun silhouette the stalks at dusk.

It's been four weeks since she told him.

"There's no baby," she announced at the door to his studio, back from a day of shopping in town. He had looked at her blankly before understanding she would make him ask, make him beg. She had been six weeks pregnant; for six weeks Reginald had kissed her brown belly and whispered into the button: "Tu madre no es normal." He had rolled his eyes up into her face and continued, smiling, "She bays at the moon. She never does the dishes. But she will teach you seven different names for the color green, and how to love madly, like a dervish."

He fixed her eggs each morning, which she pushed away in favor of coffee, and tropical salads dribbled with his signature dressing of basil and shallots. He laced her stomach with wildflowers before she woke. He spoke of building a swing set.

"He's not going to pop out running and jumping and collecting lizards, Naldo. There will be puke and no sleep for two years and lots of screaming — much more than usual," she replied. They both believed it would be a boy.

Reginald had noticed her contempt for his planning, had watched her ignore the prenatal vitamins he had picked up for her in town. He had divided them, then, into the little compartments of a pill organizer at the beginning of each week, and had checked to see that the little plastic box was empty at week's end, but a search of the trash can while she was out collecting poppies had turned up a patch of the oval white capsules in an empty can of tomato sauce. He had gone on filling the container to conceal his awareness of her subterfuge. She was easy to embarrass and expressed it with a white rage of which he had grown quite terrified.

"What do you mean?"

"I was shopping when I felt an awful pain. The clerk had to call a taxi, and I went to Dr. Salazar. It was a miscarriage." She stood for a long time, daring him to contradict her. There would be no point in

doing so. He would call Dr. Salazar later, during her siesta, and ask
vague things about his children and his ailing wife, and in the quality of
Dr. Salazar's reception of him, confirm his suspicion.

Reginald tossed his paintbrush into a pot of turpentine, strode over
to the canvas he was working on, picked it up and flung it against the
wall, where it dropped, stubbornly, without breaking. He started
toward it, then stopped, turned, and brushed past Magdalena in the
doorway without a glance. The sun was starting to set behind the
bachelor's buttons and delphiniums, and Reginald walked toward it,
trampling a line through the flowers, and straight on down the hill.

*

After the first two days, during which Magdalena had been
transparently guilty and actually cooked a chicken in lemon-and-too-
much-pepper sauce for Reginald, who ate it in silence without putting
out a cigarette, she had recovered her hearty sense of denial and began
dismantling the living room, pulling down the curtains and pushing the
sofa and chairs out into the hall. She bought red paint and started in
on the walls wearing pristine white jeans and a white t-shirt. Reginald
found her at day's end draped dramatically across the couch, slashed
with wild carnations of pigment like the victim of a bear attack. And
still he said nothing.

They carried on like this for the next weeks, the way some couples
do, living around each other but not with each other and stiffly
sidestepping the obvious presence of a third figure, a bright ghost of
regret, of accusation and sorrow and shame.

A thin reed of hate began to furrow between Reginald's brows. His
painting had gone dry. He spent whole days at Roberto's playing chess,
hunkered gratefully in the sanctum of his friend's respectful silence.

Magdalena, on the other hand, had come into bloom like one of
her poppies. Every room in the house now shone in the jewel tones of
her restlessness. She sang in the bathroom, now leafy green, to hear her
trilling bounce off the walls, and looped braids of purple garlic over the
windows in the kitchen, now a spicy yellow.

He thought of leaving, but the thought was insubstantial, had no
feet. From the moment he had seen her eating alone with a book in her
hand at a small café in Mérida, he had been fixed on her. Younger then
and possessed of the spirit of daring that comes with constant travel, he
had paused next to her on the far side of a wrought iron fence and said

in his poet's voice, "La Sirena." She had ignored him entirely. Or so he thought. Without looking up from the page, she responded in English: "To be a siren I would have to beckon to you. Instead, you are interrupting my lunch." It could have ended there, but Magdalena lifted her face and smiled like the sun giving birth to itself.

*

Edith Piaf swirls through the house, mingling with the filmy yellow light. Magdalena returns to the kitchen table and extends her hand. Reginald, softened slightly by wine, considers her pale palm. She will stand there, it seems, for as long as required. Reginald finally places his hand over hers and rises from his chair. She leads him into the crimson living room, twirls to face him and draws him firmly to her breast. She begins to sway very slowly, disregarding the heavy garland of rhythm, pressing him close but holding her face back so she can lock her eyes with his. He is rigid; she leads. They stare into one another like wolves prickling for placement in the pack, she angling their bodies in new directions but still moving slowly, he letting her take what she wants but refusing her the last thing, the thing that matters.

She jerks forward without warning and smashes her lips against his, breaking the spell. She springs back, and he breaks her grip to wipe her stain from his mouth with the back of his hand. Her eyes widen and her head wavers a little on the post of her neck. Her mouth hangs open slightly. Then, as if her bones had turned to sand, she slides down his hips, dragging at his trousers, and collapses in a heap at his knees. She is sobbing, but he remains upright, planted on the hardwood in the vise of her arms. For the first time, he imagines a day when her fleeting surrender does not move him. Even now, a part of him watches, bloodless, as he sinks to her side, inhales the sandalwood of her hair, kisses her scalp. He rubs a finger across her eyebrow, smoothing it down, and finds with some relief that she is very small, too small to hate.

Light has gone from the room. A navy blue chill has begun to spread through the house. It is time to close the windows and prepare a fire. Instead, they sit huddled in each other on the floor, two heads pressed together, a knot in the middle of darkness.

David A. Comstock

"Lying Jim" Townsend and the *Grass Valley Union*

Considering how much mileage Grass Valley has extracted from the saga of Lola Montez, it's surprising how the career of "Lying Jim" Townsend has been overlooked by historians. Like Lola, Jim was a talented, outrageous, scandalous entertainer; like Lola, he moved around a lot, felt marriage was restrictive and unnecessary, and had friends whose reputations eventually eclipsed his own. Mark Twain, Dan DeQuille, Joe Goodwin, Steve Gillis, Rollin Daggett, and Alfred Doten were among his admiring companions, and Bret Harte's earliest fame derived from a poem whose fictional narrator was modeled on Jim Townsend.

Jim's tie to Grass Valley was short-lived, thanks to a scandal of magnificent proportions. For Jim, the founding editor of Grass Valley's first Republican newspaper, betrayed his backers in his first week on the job, and sold out to the opposition party four days before a Presidential election. But why, one wonders, should that have been a surprise, given his reputation at the time.

We know now that James William Emery Townsend (Jim) was born at Portsmouth, New Hampshire, on August 4, 1838. But he always lied about his age, even to friends, and claimed to be older than he was. His father had been a sailor and so was Jim — at least to the extent that he sailed to San Francisco in 1857 as a member of the crew. Having been a printer's devil at Portsmouth, he took a job as a typesetter at the *Golden Era* newspaper, where he met up with Joe Goodman, Steve Gillis, and Bret Harte.

To entertain his companions, Jim recycled his dad's sailing stories and enlarged upon them, with himself as hero. Steve Gillis's brother Bill said Jim told them he had been forced to marry 200 Amazon maidens on a desert island. His marital duties caused him to waste away until he was a mere shadow, and one day a strong wind picked him up and blew him many miles out to sea, where he hitched a ride on a shark, rode bareback to the nearest land, and found his way back to civilization with the aid of an educated parrot.

Lying Jim soon felt the pull of the Comstock Lode. In 1862 he went to work for Joe Goodman and Denis McCarthy at the *Territorial Enterprise* in Virginia City, along with a greenhorn who had been collecting news at the mining camp of Aurora. In those days it was common practice to select a nom de plume — William Wright signed his columns "Dan DeQuille" — so the greenhorn chose "Mark Twain." Ten years later Mark Twain's first book, *Roughing It*, featured a story he had borrowed from Lying Jim:

> *This reminiscence calls to mind Jim Townsend's tunnel. He had paid assessments on a mine called the "Daley" till he was wellnigh penniless. Finally an assessment was levied to run a tunnel two hundred and fifty feet on the Daley, and Townsend went up on the hill to look into matters.*
>
> *He found the Daley cropping out of the apex of an exceedingly sharp-pointed peak, and a couple of men up there "facing" the proposed tunnel. Townsend made a calculation. Then he said to the men:*
>
> *"So you have taken a contract to run a tunnel into this hill two hundred and fifty feet to strike this ledge?"*
>
> *"Yes sir."*
>
> *"Well, do you know that you have got one of the most expensive and arduous undertakings before you that was ever conceived by man?"*
>
> *"Why no — how is that?"*
>
> *"Because this hill is only twenty-five feet through from side to side; and so you have got to build two hundred and twenty-five feet of your tunnel on trestle-work!"*

According to Joe Goodman, Jim "had a wonderful gift of original expression, and was about the biggest liar I ever knew. The reader can imagine the effect upon one of Harte's disposition of his associations with a roisterer like Townsend — a [reputed] world traveler who knew every country and every people, a free lance in all matters intellectual, a natural entertainer, with an eye for the picturesque in man and nature."

In 1870 Bret Harte wrote and published a poem Goodman and the Gillis brothers claimed was based on Lying Jim. Because the piece was about a Chinese person who outwitted some white gamblers, it was widely reprinted as "The Heathen Chinee," but Harte's own title was

"Plain Language from Truthful James." The author grew to hate the poem after it became a favorite of the anti-Chinese agitators, whom Harte despised.

Jim left the *Enterprise* in the winter of 1863-64 and went to work for the Virginia City *Union*. Little has been recorded about Townsend's marriage to Elizabeth J. "Lizzie" Lindsay, on May 1, 1864, at Dayton, Nevada. It was not a success. Within five months Lizzie was pregnant and the couple had separated. Thus, when Jim was offered an opportunity to establish a campaign newspaper at Grass Valley, California, he seems to have leapt at the chance. Jim persuaded Henry M. Blumenthal, a Virginia City stablekeeper, to join him in the enterprise and provide some cash for food and whiskey until the paper's backers came through with promised financial support.

The odds were stacked against the success of a Republican newspaper at Grass Valley, for the township was heavily Democratic, and it was bizarre to think that a new publication with strangers at the helm might affect the outcome of the fierce contest between General George McClellan and Abraham Lincoln in eleven days. Nevertheless, the two Republican dailies at Nevada City were cheered by the prospect of a voice to challenge Grass Valley's only newspaper, the *National*, which supported the Democratic candidate.

The Nevada City *Transcript*, edited by Edwin G. Waite, had reported on October 8 that a new paper would be printed with type and equipment from the *Washoe Times* in Nevada. When the first issue appeared on October 28, Waite said, "As its name indicates, it is 'Union,' and we hope it will be the means of turning some of the vile copperheads from the error of their ways."

Oliver P. Stidger, editor of the Nevada City *Gazette*, hailed its advent as "a harbinger of victory . . . . Mr. Townsend is decidedly sound on the main questions of the day, and fully comprehends the political position. We trust our Grass Valley friends and the Union men of this city and Rough & Ready township will give this paper a cordial reception and a liberal support. As for us, we welcome it into the circle of political journalism, and wish it Godspeed."

After Lying Jim paid him a friendly visit, Stidger commented with approval, "We found him an intelligent gentleman, and of course gave him a hearty welcome." Friendly remarks were rare in the campaign of 1864, and Stidger already was famous for being a prickly fellow who had survived more than his share of duels brought about by his forthright language. Typical of his confrontational style was the

harangue he published on October 31 about John Rollin Ridge, the
National editor, whose Indian father was the son of a Cherokee chief,
and whose white mother was the daughter of the principal of a school
for Indians. Stidger (who had known Ridge for many years at
Marysville) alluded nastily to Ridge's ancestry and the fact that Ridge
had fled to California after killing the man who had murdered Ridge's
father in a tribal dispute:

> *John R. Ridge, after having been denominated in the columns
> of the Gazette by every conceivable epithet that is vile and
> insulting, retorts by calling us a liar and coward. . . . As, however,
> we look upon him with contempt, he having proved himself a
> miserable, dirty sneak, and as at best he is nothing but a vile,
> degraded Indian, we cannot take any further notice of him. . . .
> The American people will not tolerate a miserable specimen of a
> degraded race, like him — a man whom our laws do not recognize
> as a citizen — to set himself up among them as a teacher of
> political duty. They have borne with the presence of this traitorous
> savage long enough. 'Tis time they put an end to his malignant
> railings against our Government and the people who support it.
> This is the very last time we shall take notice of this filthy cannibal
> scalawag.*

One day before the election Stidger's *Gazette* ran an excited story
headlined, "ATTEMPTED SWINDLE. Perfidy of a Pretended Union
Man. RIDGE, OF THE NATIONAL, AN ACCOMPLICE OF SWIN-
DLERS. A Thieving Operation Frustrated."

The story said Ridge and Townsend had tried "to perpetrate one of
the meanest swindles ever heard of." According to Stidger, Townsend had
confided to his partner Blumenthal that Ridge had offered them a bribe to
sell out to the Democratic party. Stidger said Blumenthal had refused to
take part and Townsend dropped the subject. Then Blumenthal was
approached directly by Ridge, who repeated the offer of money "if he
would raise McClellan's name at the head of his paper, and then transfer
the concern" to the Democrats. Mr. Blumenthal again refused, and told
Stidger he had said "there was not money enough in the town or the State
to hire him to do an act so mean and contemptible."

On Saturday night Lying Jim failed to show up at a meeting of the
"Lincoln and Johnson Club" he was scheduled to address in Grass
Valley. When Blumenthal went looking for Jim he found Townsend

had removed his trunk and belongings from the room they shared. At the *Union* office he quizzed Solomon Shane, an employee, who told him a deal had been made by Townsend and Ridge to transfer the paper at midnight. The printing forms of the *Union* were to be carried to the *National* office, where McClellan's name would be substituted for that of Lincoln, and a new editorial would denounce "*Union*ism." The *Gazette* revealed details of the plot:

> A thousand copies of the spurious edition were to be worked off, and the carrier of the *Union*, one Henry Waite, was to destroy the regular edition of the paper, and distribute instead to the patrons the bogus edition, prepared by Ridge. A pair of cases had already been taken to the *National* office to "set up" the infamous [editorial] written by Ridge in Townsend's name. Mr. Blumenthal caused the cases to be speedily brought back, and called in a posse of Union men to guard the office.
>
> About midnight Ridge appeared to take the forms, as per contract. Finding that the whole plot was discovered he made no secret of the matter, but claimed that, so far as he was concerned, the transaction was a perfectly fair and honorable one! . . . From some motive incomprehensible to us, the party refrained from laying violent hand on the miscreant. . . .
>
> About two o'clock Townsend came in to receive the wages of his iniquity. He was astonished at meeting, instead of the partner of his fraud, a number of indignant Union men. He affected virtuous innocence at first, but finally made a clean breast of it, asserting, however, that he had not intended to swindle his partner, but would have given him his share of the purchase money. The scamp, wonderful to relate, was permitted to depart without a horsewhipping. He has not been seen nor heard of in the neighborhood of Grass Valley, and has probably decamped.
>
> Mr. Blumenthal came yesterday to this city and engaged the services of an editor and some printers, and will make the *Grass Valley Union* a thorn in the flesh of the traitors of that town at least until after the election — we hope for a longer period. He is a true and upright Union man, and cannot be held responsible for the dishonorable conduct of his late partner. In excuse for the latter, it is said that he has been for some time partially demented on account of family difficulties.

In the same paper, Stidger castigated the Democratic editor, saying, "Ridge thinks it is 'perfectly fair and honorable' to hire a rogue to swindle his partner and betray his party. That kind of honor doubtless obtains among Indians, Confederates and thieves, but a civilized community will hardly be able to see it."

After this and similar items appeared in local papers, Ridge angrily descended on the *Union* office with two fellow Democrats, and on election day Stidger's paper carried its version of what transpired:

> A BASE ATTACK. — We learn from a reliable gentleman of Grass Valley that on yesterday morning a base attack was made by John R. Ridge upon Mr. Blumenthal of the *Grass Valley Union*, occasioned by an article published in yesterday's *Union* reflecting somewhat on Ridge for his efforts to swindle Mr. Blumenthal out of his property. . . . Ridge, in company with George D. Roberts and William S. Byrne, went to the *Union* office and found Mr. Blumenthal sitting in a chair reading. Then Ridge demanded a retraction of the article in the *Union*, which Mr. Blumenthal refused to make, whereupon Ridge struck him with a billet of wood on the side of his head, cutting a deep gash over his eye.
>
> One of the workmen in the office attempted to interfere, when Ridge drew out a pistol and pointing it toward the man threatened to shoot him if he did not stand back. After performing this chivalrous act the parties retired. . . . This is chivalry — Southern chivalry — Indian chivalry. It is just the kind of chivalry that might be expected from a man whose forefathers gloated over the death of women and children, and who carried their scalps at their belts to show the number of victims that had fallen at their hands. . . .
>
> Why the Union men of Grass Valley did not arise and hang this would-be assassin is beyond our ken. If he dared to commit such an outrageous act in this city his life would be taken on the instant. This fact he well knows, and hence the reason why he keeps clear of us.

Lincoln won in the nation, in California, and in Nevada County — but in Grass Valley township McClellan had the majority, thanks (said Republicans) to the evil alliance of Lying Jim Townsend and John Rollin Ridge.

When the *Grass Valley Union*'s 25th anniversary rolled around, Alf Doten met Jim on a train near Carson City. He said Jim was "on his way to London on account of mining trouble at Lundy." Lying Jim told others the same story, but in fact he was going only so far as the British consulate in San Francisco to testify about a mining scam at Lundy.

In 1895 Jim moved his equipment to Bodie and began publishing the *Mining Index*. He purchased the Bodie *Evening Miner* a year later and combined the two papers. When his health worsened in 1899 Townsend sold the *Miner-Index* to a pair of women employees and went to live with his married daughter in Oakland. Alf Doten met him again while en route to the Bay Area, and Jim said he would be living in East Oakland. According to Doten, Jim planned to write a book called "Truth, With Variations." Doten explained that the "truth" element would be Townsend's own "philosophical deductions from personal observation and study of the heads of mankind and their natural storage capacity for good or bad ideas." In Jim's view,

> *Heads that are never open for the reception of any new ideas or impressions are simply blockheads. Some heads close early and others close late, while the brainiest of all are always open. Then there are the men whom over-wealth or over-education has given the big-head or the swell-head, but the meanest of all is the swelled pin-head with no soul except on his feet, and dwarfed so low in the scale of humanity that he would have to stand on a brick to spit over a duck's tail. The "variations" are the readers who may dissent from Jim's peculiar ideas of truth, or consider it a case of "Jim-jams."*

Townsend suffered a paralyzing stroke at Oakland in May 1900, and died at the home of his brother John at Lake Forest, Illinois, on August 11, 1900. Lying Jim had disclosed his "actual" birthdate to Alf Doten in 1896, telling him he was born August 4, 1823. As usual, Jim was lying. His brother, who signed the death certificate, gave Jim's age as 62 years, 7 days.

The *Grass Valley Union* was not a success under Republican management. Finally its backers saw the merit of Lying Jim's example and sold it to the Democrats, who made it into a prosperous business.

Utah Phillips

The Old Guy Meets His Childhood Sweetheart

On the swing, the little girl
says, "Push."
She can't see me behind her,
small, thin, shy, the new
kid overcome with
unexplainable waves
of tenderness.
I reach out with my
pudgy hands and
touch her shoulders,
the blue frock with
puff sleeves.
I push and she swings
away from me.
"Harder."
The swing returns,
higher, my hands cup
the small of her back
and I push again.
She pumps her legs straight
out and pulls away,
the backward swing of
her hair brushing my cheek.
Up and back.
"More."
The swing, eye level now,
reaches my hands, I
press them into her
small, round hips thrust
back over the seat,
and push hard. A high
squeal of delight escapes her

as she flies away, up, up
into the sunlight; she
hangs there a long
instant and, hair swept
forward, flies back
toward my aching hands,
my tear-streaked little
face; flies back and back
through light and shadow,
spring and summer,
through page upon page
of unforgiving years,
she flies back to me.
Her hair engulfs my face.
My hands cup her hips
and she rises to me,
swinging. "Push. More."
She pumps her legs straight
out. I rise and fall like
the swing itself, soaring
into her delight.
We swing, boy and girl,
man and girl, boy and woman,
man and woman, we swing,
find, catch, hold,
remember
the sad, achingly lonely
vision of what was
wanting.
"Want to play?"
"Swing me!"
"Push."

Gail Rudd Entrekin

Deep World

Walking up our road home,
the children piling down the ravine
suddenly come scrambling back,
dust and rocks rolling and it's *something
is dead down there* as they grab
our arms and rush off, the dog
careening below them in a rattling slide.

We come slowly, picking our way,
not sure that we want to see it, this deer,
perhaps the one who ate the pink impatiens
last week from our flower boxes
or the one with her two fawns caught
in our headlights down on Silverado Trail.

Two huge turkey buzzards, their blood-red
beaks, loom above us in the bare oak branches,
their shadows moving on the muddy creek
beside the carnage — The boys go close,
cry out *its guts are spilling out!*
with such relish that we know they are stunned,
cannot believe it really. I look away.
The backbone, legs and skull are all
that will remain tomorrow. But then

the dog, *our* dog, has plunged into the mess
and stands in it. She is eating the deer.
Everyone rushes forward at once, shouting,
pulling her away. Climbing the ravine
the children look at her out of the corners
of their eyes. No one pats her. We have remembered:
She is not one of us.

The vultures, standing now by their meal,
turn back for a moment and meet our eyes:
the deep world gazing back.

Accidents

Everyone has a childhood story of
shooting their brother with a BB gun
as he climbed the tree,
thinking they would scare him,
make him curse
               or shooting their father's rifle
for the first time, straight into the soft body of a robin,
how it dropped from its branch like a stone,
stunning the child who felled it.

This is my story.
               We bought a sling shot
to scare the wild turkeys that dig in our garden,
a flock of 20 or 30 that scavenges along the road,
running wildly, ludicrously, as our car approaches,
flapping up into the lowest trees as a last resort,
all but the one who cannot fly,
the one with one leg, who hops.

Louis B. Jones

The Stone

In one of the new places north of Terra Linda, Roger Hoberman lived
with his wife Beverly and his children, Jessica and Justin, in a house on
the corner of Sunstone and Wheatstone that had almost all the
available options, including a beamed ceiling and a yard area and a
hobby nook. Roger was then the owner-manager of an unpopular and
seldom noticed Shakey's Pizza franchise, across the freeway from the
place that used to be the Holiday Inn and then got turned into offices,
on the frontage road which is for some reason always under construction, year in and year out, with great floes of weather-bleached asphalt
tipped up and striped hazard barriers blinking in the sun, scaring off
customer traffic. Inside the windowless Shakey's, where the cold
blackness swarms up to your eyes and dizzies you after the concussion
of parking-lot sunshine, Roger could be found most days between noon
and midnight. He was there, lying on his back under the bar with a
flashlight — a big man, too big for this cramped project — trying to fix
the canister of soft-drink syrup whose plastic hose had become clogged,
when he felt the first pain deep in his belly. It was a thud, a tympani-
note of pain. It made him stop work, bring his knees up a little, drop
his head gently to the concrete floor, and think about his crowded
schedule and how remiss he was in everything.

It wasn't any mortal disease. It turned out to be the first symptom
of a kidney stone. Actually the first symptom had occurred two days
earlier when Roger had run down to the Marin True Value to buy a
mop handle to replace the one broken by the new apprentice pizza
chef, and, as he was walking across the parking lot toward the store,
there was a faint sweet flush of pain in the basin of his guts, which he
ignored altogether. Roger Hoberman was a man who achieved a state
nearest to perfect mortal happiness when he was walking across
parking lots. With the slam of his car door, the flash of keys disappearing into his pocket, the unpacked spring in his stride, the renewed
consciousness of his wallet, Roger was his truest self when he was
walking toward a purchase. Or just walking. Toward anything. In

Heaven, the goal of his walking would always be just out of reach, receding into an intimate infinity while he strides with the happiness of hunger, never arriving. It's arriving that kills you. What do you get when you arrive? A mop handle. And then you stand around on the linoleum of the True Value holding this humiliating wand, awarded you as evidence that you're handling a job beneath you because others are too irresponsible, waiting for the teenager in the green True Value vest to say "May I help you?"

At forty-two, Roger was always impatient for everything to be over with. When he was at Shakey's amidst the clang of the jukebox and the silent bombs of light from the wide-screen video, while only two stingy customers dawdled over their crusts, he couldn't wait for closing time, to get back to the peace of his home. But then at home, it wasn't long before he ached to get back to the million things that needed doing at Shakey's, and he couldn't stay seated in the furniture because his muscles longed for exertion. Everything Beverly said invited contradiction irresistibly, and then he felt sorry when she gave up and merely pursed her lips. Even in bed, he lay out with the acid slime of coffee rising in his throat wishing he could fall asleep immediately by force of will. When he did get to sleep, he often dreamed about the half-acre of unimproved land he had bought way up in the cold sunshine of Mount Shasta, way outside the radii of commuter colonization of every city, where he wanted to build a cabin and sink a well, but where in fact he never visited. It was only on parking lots, only for a moment, on that great black rink where his own muscles propelled him, that Roger walked through whatever grace is, fleetingly. The hardware store turned out not to have the right kind of mop handle. All they had was tapered-end handles, and Roger needed one that was threaded, to screw into the mop.

"That's how they come," said the dull boy in the True Value vest. *Wade* was written in Ipana-blue script on it.

"What," said Roger, "I just jam it onto the mop? And after I mop the floor for five minutes, the mop falls off?"

The boy smiled. "I guess so." He was delighted.

Roger began to speak very slowly and distinctly. "And then when it falls off, do I pick it up? And jam it back onto the handle? And try to mop for another two minutes before it falls off again?"

"I guess so," said the boy, but his smile was getting filmy as he realized that this guy wasn't being humorous, and might even be weird, so that — you could see it in his fugitive eyes — Wade didn't want to be responsible here any more.

Roger said, "I'm going to have to drill this. And bolt it."

The boy averted his eyes and shifted his weight from one foot to the other. Roger cut himself off and went to the cash register and got out his wallet, his big old leather wallet thick as a bar of soap, fattened encyclopedically by receipts, Post-It notes, a matchbook cover, salesmen's business cards, jotted-on napkins, a five-dollar rebate coupon, his hole-punched Video Paradise card entitling him to a free video after twelve punches, his driver's license and credit cards and organ donor card, a mound of a wallet, old as high school, its leather burnished at the corners by the years' rub of denim, its hem warped in the pocket's humidity, curved to the shape of his gluteus maximus, all held together by a girdling, necessary rubber band. It sat on the True Value counter between them while the boy rang up the sale. Roger, through clenched teeth, valve-like, let out a sigh. And then at last he walked out of the store with his mop handle, one end of which the boy had stuck into a paper bag.

He tore off the bag and threw it into a trash can. That boy had probably never mopped a floor in his life, maybe literally never. Nobody cares about anything anymore, there's no pay-off in it. "That's how they come" is the excuse for everything. A hardware store doesn't even look like a hardware store anymore, it looks like a ladies' department store or a bookstore or a drugstore. Everything is hanging on revolving racks, packed in heat-sealed plastic on cardboard backings, so you can't even examine what you're buying. You're not supposed to care. The one guy who cares comes off looking like an asshole. Comedians on TV crack sly jokes about marijuana and cocaine, which Roger's nine-year-old doesn't yet laugh at, but someday soon she will. People have to care about things. Things mean something. Everything isn't just a pile of shit. Everything isn't just a pile of stupid shit to stand around in grinning. He knew when he got back to work, there would be the busboy's guileless torpor to face. He would be relieved the mop wasn't fixed yet. And Roger would lose an hour of his valuable time bolting the mop to the handle because he couldn't trust the boy to do it, the boy would botch it up, as if intentionally. In fact, the right bolt wasn't on the premises at Shakey's, and Roger ought to turn around right now and go back and buy one. But he kept on walking, right past his car, clutching this mop handle, because just walking felt good. And when he got to the end of the parking lot, knowing there was nowhere to go but back, he just stood there at the edge holding this stick, looking like a jerk.

When the kidney stone made itself felt for a third time, he was immobilized. It happened at Shakey's again. As in that childhood game of statues, he felt "tagged." He couldn't afford to take time off for illness, everything was so heavily mortgaged. The only thing he owned outright was the land on Mount Shasta. Slowly, slowly, imperceptibly, he set down the *SuperSlurp!* paper cup he was holding in the gaudy dark, and one of the employees folded him into the passenger seat of the car and drove him to the Kaiser Medical Center. It was a kidney stone, X-rays immediately showed. The doctor (His eyes never once met Roger's) was so flippantly bored by Roger's problem that his professional touch — on Roger's elbow, spine, breast, throat — was divine, angelic. And the valley of Terra Linda flooded with God's intentions again, of course. Surgery wouldn't be necessary, renal calculi are irritating as all get-out, but never fatal, the only thing to do was take it easy, be patient, relax, and eventually the stone would be passed in urination. It was a tiny grain that had crystallized over the years. As a fact, that was astonishing. A stone had grown inside him, and it would emerge from his very penis. He was instructed to urinate into a fine mesh sieve. The doctor handed him a prescription, which he carried in his hand like valuable new currency, like a ticket to some-where, as he rode back to work in a taxi-cab, slightly alienated now from the place he'd grown up in passing like scenery. Then at Shakey's, he drove his own car home and — feeling perfectly fine now — clipped the prescription with a magnet to the refrigerator in the kitchen, calling out, "Hey, Beverly."

She wasn't home. He was angry with her for not being home. She was always home. After pacing around the empty house for some time, he settled down at the hobby nook in the garage where paperwork piled up, a mountain of evidence that the Shakey's was failing, base-ment-clammy, frigid with air-conditioning, too heavily mortgaged. In spite of his medical condition, he could make efficient use of his time. Indeed, he was well into the pleasant, coffee-enhanced trance of miscellany when Beverly's familiar Toyota sound interrupted him. She would have seen his car in the driveway. But then there was some pausing outside in the carport, some tenderness in opening the front door, some pausing again in the kitchen, before at last she called, "Roger! You're home!" and the totally fantastic certainty crossed his mind that she was having an affair. It was decreed by the tarot he'd spread before him, of unpaid bills. She called out, "What's this?" because she'd found the prescription on the refrigerator. It made him instantly angry, her asking. He didn't answer. He just stared down at the computerized HandiKup bill on the work bench, his pen poised in air.

She appeared in the doorway beside him, puzzling over the Sanskrit on the slip. "Roger, what is this?"

"Oh, that. Nothing. Something from the doctor." It was all so annoying he was almost blind.

"What's it for?"

"I have a kidney stone. OK? It's no big deal. I went to the doctor, and he said I have a kidney stone."

She stayed in the doorway. The HandiKup bill swam beneath his vision.

"A kidney stone. Don't people *remove* those?"

"No, they just go away. Look, I'm right in the middle of this. Could we talk later? It's no big deal. It will go away in a few weeks."

"A few weeks," said Beverly, standing there ruminating as this stone took shape in her mind. She drew breath to ask another question but then didn't. Vanished silently from the doorway. Giving up on him again. Good-bye, good-bye. Soon the radio came from the kitchen, that easy-rock station she loved so much. She always loved music. The sound of a paper grocery bag. He remembered her in high school, how she loved music then too, which seemed sad. Regret, at a certain point in life, involves a hard swallowing motion. He could picture her reaching up on tiptoe to put cans on the top shelf: her calf, her thigh.

* * *

Over the weeks the crystal kept looking for the passage of exit, creeping down, but then it would be driven back by the ejaculatory spasm of pain. He tried to go on at the Shakey's for a while, but the pains kept creating awkward situations. That inner cord would yank tight, and he would double over. Once, the styrofoam "straw hat" (which he and all the employees were required by Shakey's International by-law to wear at all times) fell off and knocked a Coke into a customer's lap. Driving was dangerous because if the pain came back when he was on the freeway he might not be able to lift his foot to the brake pedal. "Honey," said Beverly, lying beside him in bed with the *TV Guide*, "Couldn't you let one of the older kids there manage the place for you? Why do you have to be there all the time?" At this point, the stone had dwelt within him for six weeks. It wasn't going as easily as the doctor had hoped.

"Those kids," said Roger in answer.

She tossed onto her side toward him, nudged by an idea with all her fake happiness. "Couldn't Shakey's International send a manager out, temporarily?"

"It has to be me. It's my franchise. Stop making the bed jiggle." But there was something else. He was in debt. He had borrowed heavily to make the down payment on the franchise, and he had taken out a second mortgage on the house. When customers came in, looked around the empty place and decided to stay, he would put on his styrofoam hat, light as popcorn, and appear like a puppet behind the bar saying merrily, "Howdy, folks — Y'in the market for a pizza?" and start swabbing down the bar, as if he'd just opened up, as if these were only the first guests arriving at what would be a large party. But of course the party never materialized. If the customers didn't put a quarter in the jukebox, they would eat their pizza within the melancholy rumble of the kitchen equipment, the roar of refrigeration that held them all, him, them, the two employees leaning against the counters soaking up their minimum wage, the huge oven drinking up electricity that made the aluminum disk with the calibrated rim, out back in the utility company's meter, whirl and whirl and whirl, measuring.

"Bev, it doesn't work that way," he told her, revolving himself gently away from her on the mattress, onto his side. "Just don't try to help, okay?"

That put an end to it, and she went back to the *TV Guide*. But a minute later he made the mistake of holding his breath, expecting a pang — which never came — so that Beverly noticed. She said, "You haven't had your cranberry juice tonight, have you?"

"Fuck the cranberry juice. I hate that goddamn cranberry juice."

She didn't say anything. Then she got up and put on her robe.

Roger heard her in the kitchen opening the refrigerator, pouring a tall glass of the juice the doctor had prescribed a daily gallon of. He recognized the clink of the nice Crate & Barrel glassware. Then for a long while there was silence. She seemed to be just standing alone in the kitchen. His heart went out to her. That his intuition was right — that she was having an affair with a twenty-five-year-old named Jacques — was something he found out only later. But even now there was a persistent sense of a missing piece, an uncrossed borderline in the vicinity, or of her taking colder breaths alone in other rooms. When she appeared in the doorway with the scarlet glass of juice she was smiling, with only a faint rubbed-redness about the eyes. "Now drink this," she said. "If we don't do what the doctor says, how can we make you better?"

According to the lab tests, the stone was probably composed of calcium oxalate minerals. He supposed it was like the sliding gravel that accumulates over the years in a tea kettle. Its crystalline structure had sharp edges that kept getting caught as it bumbled blindly towards birth. The doctor prescribed a drug, Penicillamine, which was supposed to dissolve it; but the side effects were nausea and dizziness, as well as severe diarrhea. Roger couldn't go to the Shakey's at all. He dwelt within a dim den at home where the children ventured only with a shyness and fearfulness as if they were visiting a dying dragon. In their pajamas after their baths, glowing through the dusk of his nausea, they appeared in the posture of bashful acolytes for the ceremony of "saying goodnight to Dad," and then he waved them away into the world. Beverly kept bringing him, like red candles, offerings of cranberry juice, and then — when the doctor changed his mind, deciding that his system should be extremely alkaline — cloudy baking soda potions. There would be lucid periods when the miasma would lift, during which he might put on a robe and prowl the house tipped slightly forward, waiting for the pain to trip him. But the drug-induced dizziness would always rise back up around him and he would make his way back to the den, grasping swimmingly at passing furniture.

He slept alone on the den couch now because Beverly jiggled the bed too much. Her motions in his vicinity were clumsy and apologetic. She was beautiful, from this remove, her clumsiness was beautiful, and behind a distancing teardrop lens he fell in love with her again. He actually stopped worrying about the Shakey's, which was rapidly failing under the management of a Shakey's International "troubleshooter." According to the faint and refracted rays of news that penetrated Roger's den, a new trainee had left the ovens on all night, set on "high," so that there was a small fire during the night. But Roger was so seasick, it was difficult to care much. When the Shakey's representative called one day to say that his franchise had been cursed with a bad location from the very beginning and that the San Rafael bank that carried his loans was going to "attach" the premises and liquidate everything, Roger told him that he couldn't think about it, and he hung up the phone gently, with an odd sense of victory. He laid his head on the pillow and went under again.

* * *

It was two weeks later that "Jacques" was discussed. Beverly had left home in the morning, saying she would be spending the day at her mother's house in Santa Rosa. Then in the afternoon her mother happened to phone and it came out during the conversation that Beverly wasn't there. A number of unaccountable absences and silences now arranged themselves logically in Roger's mind. When she came home that evening he watched her — her adulterousness a kind of unmentioned sunburn on her face — and found himself withering with compassion, crippled in his usual kitchen chair, as if it were all his fault. After dinner when the children were safely enfolded within the sound of gunfire and reckless driving on the TV sound track, Roger sat in his vinyl swivel chair while Beverly rinsed dishes. She made small talk. Her hands made healing motions as she laved each cup and plate in water. Finally, in a lull, Roger said with his heart pounding, "Your mother called today."

"She did," Beverly said mildly, drying off her hands. "Just a sec." And she went into the bedroom. Roger heard the bathroom door close. For a long time he waited. He knew she was crying in there. He stood up to go to talk to her, and he realized the stone was making progress again, working its way down into the dangerous zone where, in a spasm, it might be bitten back up into his insides again, losing what it had gained, so he walked carefully into the bedroom and leaned against the bathroom door trying to relax himself as much as possible, trying to imagine himself a slack chute of exit.

With his forehead leaning against the closed bathroom door, he said, "Beverly?"

No sound within.

"Beverly?" he said. "It's OK."

There was no reply. Roger turned around and leaned his back against the bathroom door.

"Really, Bev. It's OK. I mean it's understandable."

After a minute Beverly said in horror, "It's understandable!" He'd said the wrong thing.

"I mean I understand. I mean it makes sense."

"It makes sense?" she said, her voice beginning to wobble. Why was this making things worse? He turned around again to project his voice through the door. "I'm trying to tell you you shouldn't feel bad, honey. I mean, I'm aware that I'm not exactly . . ." (Not exactly what? Not exactly Mister Wonderful these days?)

"Exactly what?" said Beverly, her voice not at all weepy, suddenly dry with alarm. "You're not exactly what?"

But Roger couldn't answer: he was making a slow-motion lunge to sit down on the bed, anticipating a pain, which was announced by the familiar contraction — but which luckily never came.

Beverly opened the bathroom door, holding a box of Kleenex in her hand, and said softly, "You're not exactly what?"

He couldn't answer for a minute. She could see that. She sat down on the bed beside him, but at a slight distance, leaving a gap big enough for this invisible person to sit between them.

"Who is he? I mean, whoever he is, I'm sure he's a nice guy."

Beverly sighed. She was pleating an edge of a Kleenex against her thigh, hemming it.

She answered at last, "It's nobody you know. I'd rather not tell you."

"What do you think? I'll find him and beat him up? I just want to know his name."

She kept pleating the tissue all the harder. "Jacques," she said. "You don't know him."

"Jacques?" said Roger.

She didn't say anything.

After a moment, he said, "Mm."

"What do you mean, 'mm'?"

"Nothing."

But she was looking at him. He sighed. "Just the name, 'Jacques.' You get a picture of him. What does he do?"

"He's a recording engineer."

"Yeah and I bet he writes songs too."

"Oh, Roger."

She looked at him, then stopped looking at him and started tearing little notches in her Kleenex. There was a long silence. She tucked her knees up under her chin and hugged her shins. She said, "But Roger, I love you. I want you. He's not . . . He's okay, he's nice, but he's not . . ."

Roger said, "I know."

She hugged her knees tighter.

After a while, she said, "This is happening at the wrong time."

"I know."

She sighed and rubbed her ear on her kneecap. "I've been trying to get rid of him. Actually, it was stupid. Actually, as a matter of fact, you wouldn't like him."

"No, it wasn't stupid."

"Yes, it was," she said, and the tears started to come.

That night they lay fully clothed side by side on the bed, both waiting, as if to see where the bruise would rise or how exactly it would bloom. The expectancy was something they shared now, like a young couple at the beginning of their marriage. The children were asleep.

Roger started. "I'm going to owe a lot of money on the Shakey's thing. I think we'll probably have to sell the house."

"OK."

"I was borrowing on the house to cover the franchise payments."

"OK."

"But Bev?"

"What."

"Would it be OK if we separated? Just for a bit? Do you think that's a good thing to do?"

"Well, why?"

He didn't want to think about why; or even know why.

"We'll be fine," he said.

* * *

The pain had started to come with such frequency that, at night, he never really sank to the deeper levels of sleep but it kept yanking him back up to the surface on its embedded hook. So in the day his bones ached from tiredness, and the ring of his attention shrank and bulged so that he could only focus on immediate and present objects: a countertop, a bowl of cereal, a document from Shakey's International to be signed, a picture Jessica had drawn in school — as if he were limited to viewing life through the queasy viewfinder of that old childhood Viewmaster of his, whose plastic against his nose smelled like comfort while pictures of unattainable icy mountain peaks revolved under the squeeze of his finger. Cowering in the den, he was only peripherally conscious of the real estate agent's voice, which said, "Excuse us, just for a minute, Mr. Hoberman. Folks, this is the recreation room, but it could serve as a child's bedroom, this is Mr. Hoberman," addressing prospective buyers who filed past always reverent like gentiles in some weird mosque. It got so he didn't even lift his eyes. When Beverly had packed him into the Toyota and driven him to the Kaiser Medical Center for one of his consultations, the doctor sat down and clicked his tongue meditatively, reviewing a computer print-out of test results, and then said, "Roger, I think it might be time for us to go in."

"Go in?"

"The prevailing philosophy is to stall off surgery as long as possible, but this has been going on for too long. It's taking a toll on your system."

Roger didn't say anything.

The doctor said, "Really, it's too bad. There's a technology in development involving high-frequency sound waves that will just explode renal calculi in vivo. But that's years off."

Roger still didn't say anything, guiltily, stubbornly, congealing within.

"Let me just describe this operation."

"No," said Roger. "No surgery."

The doctor leaned back in his tilting chair. "Well, I'm recommending surgery."

"No. I want to go on with this."

Beverly hired an accountant, whom Roger gave power of attorney over his affairs, because in his present exalted weariness he couldn't think about it. He only had to sign an occasional document that Beverly would slide into the shrinking circle of his field of consciousness. As more home-buyers kept trooping through the house, he started to feel more and more like a discovered squatter on the premises and it became clear he and his family would have to clear out.

"Well," Beverly said, "there's always my mother's place. The kids love it up there. She'd be glad to have us. Since Dad, she's just been rattling around."

"Fine," Roger said. They were sitting side by side on the living room couch in the jerky light of the television. Beverly had cut the sound track with the remote control unit. They both faced the screen. She said, "We could put all this stuff in storage. It won't be too expensive. And if we do it now, Jessica and Justin can start the school year fresh in Santa Rosa."

"OK," said Roger.

After a silence, while the image on the screen zoomed and smashed, Roger said, "But Bev? I'll move into a motel."

She stood up to go to the kitchen. Then she came back and stood in the doorway silhouetted against the kitchen's fluorescent lights. She said, "It's this thing, isn't it," shrugging her delicate shoulder toward her own ongoing penitence. She seemed to want penitence. There was no way of saying to her how irrelevant that was. People have to want what they want. And get what they get.

"No," he said.

She said, "What motel? For Christ's sake, Roger. You're too sick to be alone."

"The Bermuda Palms," said Roger. "I'll be fine. I can mix my own bicarbonate of soda. And I'll always be within six feet of a telephone. They have a monthly rate. I called them. I've thought about this."

"I see." She started to bite a cuticle, holding one elbow in the palm of her hand, and she leaned against the door jamb. She set one foot atop the other, the way she always did.

"I love you," Roger said.

* * *

Nothing in the motel room was his, except for the open suitcase on the floor in the corner under its heap of clothes. Even his old wallet, rubber-band-encircled, was stored away in the boxes of stuff in his mother-in-law's garage in Santa Rosa, so that when he took his short limping walks around the seedy neighborhood of the motel, his pockets were empty. The new circumstances of his life — the telephone without a dial, the small wrapped soap, the stiff sheets and rough granular towels, the sandpaper daisies stuck to the tub's floor, the view outside onto the motel's grimy marquee announcing waterbeds and cable TV — everything provided the pleasant abrasion of anonymity. It was his cure. He spent most of the time sitting on the floor. The constant ache focused his mind. Sometimes he was interrupted by the accountant phoning to say the buyers for his house had arranged financing, or that Shakey's International had paid the first installment of his franchise return, or that the land on Mount Shasta had been sold at a loss, or that State Farm's cashed-in policy had paid a small refund; or Beverly came by with the kids, who fidgeted and brought him small rehearsed bulletins from kindergarten or the playing field — but mostly his head was raised in visualizing a very specific pain as he sat alone on the floor. The yarns of the carpet were waxy with the sweet filth of the freeway filtering in over the years. His fingers idly plucked and whorled the nap of it. The pain was steady, a boulder. And then at times there was the ecstasy, the orgasmic scoop. It made him stagger up. The bathroom's white porcelain, cool as heaven, loomed toward him. He never turned off the bedside lamps. He had stopped sleeping and waking at the usual hours. Day or night, he would doze for periods, kneeling or cross-legged. What was sleeping, what waking? If the pain let up for a while he might walk out to the 7-Eleven on the corner.

When he thought of Beverly he wished he could get a message to her, that he loved her. Then the rough twine in his guts kept jerking, and he would lurch up towards porcelain. If he imagined this agony going on and on indefinitely, he pictured himself outside in the shelter of the rear wall of the 7-Eleven — there was something almost cozy about the picture — hunkering down among the diamonds of shattered windshield glass and the concrete tire-stops where the south sun gets warm even in winter. And then when the pain came back, he couldn't think about anything for a while. The floor of the bathroom rose up, a raft he could cling to, cool on the forearm, the forehead. The pain kept pushing at his middle until, like bliss, it made him stop resisting it and go limp and let it stir him and fold him. Bracing himself, he was a stanchion in the earth. And then suddenly it was over. It was a translucent grain that held the light. He fell asleep as soon as he saw it, dreamlessly, on the bathroom floor. When he woke up, he remembered he had passed the stone. It was all over. He sat up slowly, with a sensation of brokenness, and of mending.

He got up on his feet, testingly, and felt just fine. He pushed his shoulders back, away from the habitual curve of molding himself around the boulder. Which had now disappeared. Everything was before him. How quiet everything was. He put on some new clothes, which rustled.

It was a tiny dull jewel, not so sharp-edged as he'd imagined. A soft dawn was trapped inside. Carrying it in his hand in his pocket, he walked out his door and into the parking lot. It felt like mid-morning, judging by the sun angle and the activity in the neighborhood. But he didn't know which day of the week. He started walking in the direction of the freeway carrying the stone in his hand. What should he do with it? He could save it in a jar and show it to people, ridiculously. Or just throw it away: just toss it in the construction site beside the freeway, where it would be churned under in the original surf of earth. He wanted to show it to Beverly, which was probably ridiculous. He just kept walking, diagonally out of the parking lot, north toward the freeway, epaulets of sun on his shoulders weighting him to relaxation. If he kept walking along the frontage road, he would eventually go past the Shakey's, now owned by somebody else. The smell of the earth of the construction site in the warm sun rose to him like fresh-baked bread, and he stopped at the curb of the frontage road and just stood there, at the edge of the freeway, holding out in the palm of his hand this new stone.

Karla Arens

Graniteville Night

All I wanted through the long, soggy spring was this —
to lie outside in the bright summer night

in a circle of trees and look up through
the chocolate dark forest at the stars.

I must have poked you awake a dozen times or more
whispering into the musky azalea air,

"Look at the stars, look at the stars,"
then sat up to listen

as if to hear the crackle of stars
a million years from here, as if

to feel the splitting of the milky bark of firs
the star's white quickening in wood.

Charles Entrekin

The First Television

> *That which does not kill us*
> *will make us stronger . . .* F. Nietzsche

My mother's twin sister Ethel and her "low-class" husband, Gaither
Lee (a large, red-faced man who could eat white onions raw and drink
whiskey straight from the bottle) had jumped ahead of our family in
importance because they had gone out and purchased their own
television set. I'm not sure which fact amazed us more: that there really
was such a thing as "television" or that Gaither Lee and Ethel had
gotten one ahead of us. And Marvin and I, ages five and seven respectively, could barely stand still we were so dazzled by the news being
passed on to us by our mother. Mom was the one who gave us the real
information concerning family plans, destinations, and changes in
status. We were getting all dressed up because we were going over to
Ethel's to see their new television set.

That summer in Birmingham, Alabama, 1949, I was standing on
our screened-in front porch in the heat, suffering a starched shirt that
itched and watching Mom put her finishing touches on Betty Ann, age
four, while Dad, wearing a tie and white shirt, held Stephen Michael,
age nine months. We were dressed up not because we were going to
church but because it was Sunday and everybody else would be dressed
up.

That year we owned a squarish, blue-gray, four-door Plymouth
with brown interior and back door handles that opened outwards by
pushing down instead of pulling up. Dad, recently hired by Southern
Bell Telephone as a line repairman, had just bought it. Mom still didn't
know how to drive. So we were going to take our new car out for a
spin, and we were going to get to go to Ethel's to see Gaither Lee's
brand new television.

Maybe it was the excitement of the proposed visit but more
probably it was the simple animus of brothers that pushed us over into

the fight that caused all the trouble. It was likely caused by something about sitting next to the open window in order to spit at the mailboxes at the bottom of the hill. And our fights had a way of escalating beyond control. I always thought I could manage Marvin, and sometimes I could, but sometimes Marvin, without warning, would tip our disagreements over into all-out war. I think he thought I was trying to take advantage of him. So suddenly, without warning, we would have to fight.

Well, once we got going, naturally we completely forgot about Betty Ann, who was actually the one sitting by the window. And then Marvin and I, locked up like two cats that could give no quarter, began pushing and grabbing and rolling about in the back seat. And Betty Ann, who had been sitting quietly in all innocence beside us, began to try to squirm out from under our maelstrom. I vaguely remember her new shiny black shoes and a short print dress that tied in the back as one remembers something seen but not focused on. She was four, barely human.

Anyway, Betty Ann, attempting to escape the action by slipping under our writhing forms, had leaned away from us while holding onto the door-handle. We never even noticed her. I had broken loose from Marvin's grip and shoved him, even as he was still trying to catch and hold onto me, onto the other side of the car, and then Betty Ann just disappeared. Somehow, as the car took a turn, the door swung open with Betty Ann holding on, and then slammed closed again, and Betty Ann was gone.

Marvin and I recognized her absence almost immediately. We stopped fighting and stared at each other. Then, without a word between us, we leaped up onto the back seat to look out the window. And there she was rolling down the hill behind us.

Marvin and I both screamed, "Dad!"

For a long moment nothing seemed to happen. Then suddenly the car lurched to a stop, and Marvin and I were thrown backwards against the front seat. Then, in slow motion, we watched Dad leap out of the car and begin hurrying toward Betty Ann. But halfway there, he abruptly stopped as if he'd reached the end of an invisible string, turned, almost falling down, and began, face grim with determination, to chase after us.

Our car had begun rolling forward, driverless, down the hill. Dad had forgotten to set the emergency brake, and Mom and Stephen Michael were screaming.

Marvin and I leaped up, wide-eyed, to watch as Betty Ann struggled to her feet by herself, and, crying out with arms and hands extended, began to chase after Dad, who was now chasing after us.

At the last driveway before the intersection, Dad managed to run along beside the careering car, jump in, pull up on the emergency brake, and then turn the wheels into the curb. We came to a stop on a neighbor's driveway and front lawn. Then Betty Ann caught up, and Dad was examining her in his arms. Marvin and I became very quiet. We might not get to see the television.

* * *

Back at the house, we sat on the front steps as Mom and Dad decided what to do. Dad said, "Well, Ruth, what do you think? Should we go or not?" As usual, it was Mom who made these final decisions. So Mom turned, and with her we all turned back to Betty Ann. Mom asked her, "How do you feel, honey?"

There was a long quiet pause. Betty Ann looked up, her face still puffy from crying. A big bump and angry-looking scratch marks on one side of her face made her look a little sad and lopsided, and she was completely dirty except where tears had streaked down her cheeks.

"I was scared you were going to leave me."

She was going to be all right.

* * *

Somehow actually seeing our first television did not live up to expectations. Gaither Lee's television screen was very small, with lots of black and white test patterns and a loud tuning-in signal that was an electronic whistle in the middle of a white noise of static. And then it offered "The Howdy Doody Show" to all of us in their small living room, the television on one side and a large fan on the other. There were Ethel and Gaither Lee and cousin Dink in his wheelchair, slumped over, his too-large encephalitic head and crossed eyes staring at you and wanting you to talk to him, and cousins Linda and Joan with their little-girl laughter, running around and giggling. After the first show we waited a long time for more test patterns to go away, then watched another show, and then went out to play.

I climbed their chinaberry tree to lie back on a branch and be alone and watch the clouds take on different shapes. Betty Ann was wild the rest of that day, as if her near extinction hadn't fazed her. I looked down from my perch as she ran in her little-girl dress back to the house. And as I watched her open the door and disappear inside, I thought about it all again. The sudden recognition of her absence had felt like something had been dropped and would turn out to be broken. One moment she had been there, the next gone. It worried me, but it wasn't a big worry. It was a worry I could think about only a little at a time, like trying to find something I know I can find if I look for it out of the corner of my eye, like locating a rabbit standing still in high grass . . .

And then Marvin called for me to come in. There was something really funny happening on television.

Hay Stacker

Too small to lift a pitch fork full from
below, I would climb up top and catch each throw,
mid-air, then guide and drop the load in one motion,
until the wagon would hold no more.
　　　　　Then coming out of the dust from the back four acres
I'd be atop the hay, barely able to breathe in the heat,
yet lying back in the wet of my own sweat, almost complete.
　　　　　And when we passed beneath the big pear tree
there in the middle of my grandfather's pasture,
I knew how it would be:
I would stick out my hand and
take the pear straight out of the air,
without effort; it would come to me
because it belonged to me.
　　　　　I hadn't yet guessed how things could go wrong,
or how it might be to be left alone, or that one
could lose badly and go down at the end
like my mother, shaking and defeated.
　　　　　I was, in that moment, simply there
watching my cousins and uncles in the distance, shimmering
in the hot air like mirages in black rubber boots,
with pitchforks in hand,
　　　　　and when I took my first dusty bite,
　　　　　it was like my first
sinking deep into a woman's body,
almost overwhelming, and I could feel
　　　　　the pear's juice sinking into me
as I lay there in the hay-scented air, adrift
and becoming everything around me,
　　　　　until suddenly I laughed out loud
　　　　　without knowing
what the laughter was about
as it poured out of me
at the top of the tree-high stack
while the future waited,
and I was carried on the harvest to the barn.

Fall

Molly Fisk

Kindness

Halfway through our nap the rain begins, hits the window,
splashes through the double-needled pines, and splurts down

onto the mules' ears and Rein orchids, the clustered blue-faced
penstemons, sinking without a trace into the granite soil.

I roll gently out from under his arm and watch him sleeping the sleep
of the sunburned, of the good son, the wall-primer and painter,

the sleep of a man who is truly tired and knows someone
loves him, since I unaccountably began to cry about it over lunch

and couldn't stop, watching him eat was suddenly
too much for me, thinking how easily he could have died

in that fall, how he wandered lonely in the wilderness of his own mind,
never mind that people cared for him, for so long, twenty years,

long enough for me to get my second wind, to begin again
to grow up, so that I recognized true love when I saw it, looked

beyond the gnarled teeth and broken nose, the central, equatorial scar
that runs his length from trachea to pubis, beyond the lost names

and repeated stories into kindness, so that when he began the steep
climb out of his brainpan's maze into stronger light, how lucky

I was there at the top of the stairs, passing by.

For the Plants Left Unplanted

Waiting is all there is in between rain and early morning sun
and a cat asleep on the bare dirt under your lowest branches.

He is also waiting, dreaming of lizards, the big black moths
that float over lavender, wallflowers, columbine,

and fling themselves into the porch light's shallow bowl
while you are watching the stars and dreaming the rooting

dream of damp soil as far as you can grow, worms
that pull you dark and down, the growing dream

when your branches extend past the picket fence, the eaves,
the nearest maple, and shelter congregations of birds,

titmice and towhees and black-headed grosbeaks. You wake
to thin light and rain on your leaves, rain slowly filling

the black plastic basin you live in.

At Home on the Page

When I got my MBA back in the early '80s, I had every intention of using it. MBAs are expensive and useful degrees, after all, and most people don't go to business school just for a lark. I really thought I wanted to be a banker. I wanted to work in a big place and be one of many; I wanted to make money; I wanted to follow my father into the business world. After I discovered that I would never speak finance like a native, I tried small business consulting, which was a little too much like being a therapist. Next I worked as a contract investigator for the Equal Employment Opportunities Commission, which was still like being a therapist but it was very PC and it paid better.

I was still miserable. Then one day I came across a contemporary book of poems — Mary Oliver's *American Primitive* — and poetry washed over me in a cool wave. A tidal wave, as it turned out, because my life has never been the same. For reasons I cannot explain, poetry turned out to be my native tongue. Its combination of words and silence spoke to me as nothing else had ever done and completely opened my heart. So despite the nonexistent pay scale and extremely marginal reputation, not to mention my Wall Street friends' ribald remarks about goatees and black turtlenecks, I became a poet.

The poems I wrote were soaked in the smells and sounds of California's north coast, where I lived then, in a minuscule village sandwiched between two national parks. Words like *kelp* and *tide* and *egret* were as common in my work as the color blue — from the ladder of darkening blues that the sky climbs down in twilight to the metallic slate blue of early morning when sunlight first greets the ocean.

I spent five happy years writing about my seaside world — including the whale that washed up on shore one spring, the backhoe that came to bury it, and the second backhoe that had to fish the first one out of the hole where it had fallen in on top of the whale. I wrote poems about the bartenders and the park rangers, and every bird I could identify with Peterson's guide. I dedicated my first book, *Salt Water Poems*, to my village, "post office, stop sign, tide line and all." Then I fell in love with a man who lived in the foothills of the Sierra Nevada, 200 miles inland and 2500 feet above sea level, and I left the landscape where I'd learned to see what truly matters, where I'd become my real self.

Since love completely addles your brain, it didn't dawn on me until months after my move to Nevada City — its landscape riddled with old mines from California's Gold Rush instead of the World War II bunkers that dotted my rocky coastline — that I wasn't looking forward to writing anymore. I've always written in the early mornings, sitting in bed or on the sofa. Now the bed was occupied by someone snoring, which, after I wrote about that a couple of times, turned out to be uninspiring, and his sofa was too squishy to sit in and write. Instead, poems came to me most often in rest stops on Interstate 80 on my way home from visiting friends on the coast. I wrote a lot of lines about oleanders blooming in the median strip and the dusty yellow flowers that thrive by the side of the road. Fast food restaurants, strip malls, billboards for gambling casinos in Reno, and double yellow lines crept into my stanzas, along with a new kind of alienation. In my writing and in my life, I felt between two worlds, misplaced.

At the same time I was struggling with my poetry and the complexities of true love, however, I stumbled into some literary nooks and crannies — a *lot* of them — in my new town. One day I learned that both Mark Twain and Bret Harte had lived here during the Gold Rush and are considered local heroes. Another night a friend dragged me to a poetry reading in a wooden cabin in someone's back yard, where I sat in an audience of 50, huge even by San Francisco or Berkeley standards.

I tried to join a book group and found out that all of the groups that meet regularly were filled. (Waiting lists for a *book group* in this technological age?) Some are of such exclusivity and long-standing that my friend Tom (who was born and raised here) inherited his mother's slot when she died. He now spends one night a month with 15 nonagenarians, deep in discussion of Stefan Japrisot's *A Very Long Engagement* or Molly Gloss's *Jump-Off Creek*. And the day I first went to soak my toes in the Yuba River (what they have here instead of the ocean), I took along a copy of the locally published eco-literary quarterly, *Wild Duck Review*, and had my preconceived notions about rural writing figuratively doused with some very cold water.

As my love-fogged thinking began to clear, I noticed that I had somehow managed to move to a tiny corner of the Sierras with 24 bookstores, none of them larger than Jimmy Stewart's bank office in *It's a Wonderful Life*. That many bookstores in two small towns — Nevada City and neighboring Grass Valley — whose combined population is only 7,400, is a miracle. There are no Barnes & Nobles here — for those you have to drive an hour south to Sacramento — and the only reason you would need to is to buy the *Southeast Asian Wall Street Journal* or the *London Sunday Times.* Here, along with the usual new books, you have Californiana, Celtic lore, and an entire business devoted to out-of-print geography books.

And there was more. The October weekend I had arrived in my 18-foot U-Haul (no exercise equipment or dining room sets here — the baggage poets carry is in their heads) had marked the first annual Wordslingers Festival, a giant shindig invented by local readers, writers, and booksellers to celebrate "the word." As I crept nervously down Nevada City's steep main drag, standing on the brakes and praying that I wouldn't sideswipe the police chief, who was double-parked outside the station, I didn't know that more than 20 poets, writers, storytellers, and singer-songwriters were performing all over town. They filled the Odd Fellows Hall, the auditorium of a public grade school, the Stone Hall of the old Miner's Foundry that's been made into a museum, and the basement enclave of the Veterans of Foreign Wars — all reading something related (sometimes very tangentially) to the theme words *mud* or *redemption.*

It took me almost a year (that's about when the dizziest stage of love wore off) to discover I'd moved to a writer's idea of heaven. True, it will never be the coast, although I've discovered that — if you squint — large parking lots sort of look like the ocean. But in typical cosmic fashion, it's the universe's idea of a *really* good consolation prize. There are readings almost every week on community radio, in the bookstores, on the local cable channel. You can't cross the street without tripping over someone who's going to the Yucatan for two weeks to study memoir, or somebody else who's taking a three-day metaphor class from a local novelist. I teach poetry now in my living room every Monday morning (which gives me an unassailable reason to vacuum on Sunday nights). My students range in age from 30 to 80. They aren't trying to become famous poets. They're here because they love words and love the world around them and want to make something of the two.

As it turns out, in Nevada City writing is a calling. Even though I'm extremely small potatoes in the writing world, when I step out onto Broad Street headed for the store to buy a light bulb, people smile and wave and ask what I'm working on. It's very encouraging, which I badly need because poets make no money to speak of, and, if they're even known to the average citizen, are usually considered either savants or tetched in the head. To have what I do valued the way it is here — by my car mechanic, banker and nurse practitioner as well as by fellow writers — makes me feel like Homer instead of Gomer Pyle.

This year is the Gold Country's 154th anniversary. The Wordslingers Festival is still going strong. In my writing you can now find *granite* and *blistering heat* and *sugar pine*. But mostly I write about love, which got me here, to this little Victorian picture postcard built by miners, almost forgotten, and then reawakened by words.

Christine Irving

Of Moths & Their Ear Mites

Moths fly their night ways,
fat wings furred to muffle flight,
sharp ears alert to shrilling squeaks,
evading the whistling swoop of bats.

Baby mites begin their lives
born on moth's shoulder, curled tight
inside infinitesimal shells.

They hatch into hunger,
directed by dreams to mewl
through buffbrown thickets.

The first mite to leave the nest
decides the course for all the rest
choosing one direction: left or right,
exudes a nectar so provocative,
so sweet, his siblings
cannot deviate.

Safe inside, they feast,
nibbling on tender whorls and ridges,
scuttling tiny feet across the tympani.

One ear alone goes deaf.
The cock-eared moth
flies on to meet and mate.
I have no notion
how mites propagate.

Gregg Wiltshire

It Meant

It meant so
        very
             very
when I found
        you
           as
               moved
by our moving
          as
             much
                 much
as I.

For when we met,
           there,
               fast,
                   first
inside my chest
          perching
              pensive
                   birds.
Then,

shower of stones
          cast
            by
              you
sudden to air
         burst,
            then
              wing
released me.

So when you
            left,
                  no
                        reason,
I became undone,
                  and
                        do
                              not
again ever
            wish
                  wish
                        to
repeat you.

Gary Short

Psalm

The sky is the red of the healing wound
of St. Agatha. New light
cast on the seven dead geese
stacked in the bed of the truck.
Their wings stiff around their bodies
make them cocoons of former flight.

The boy's breath, like a white wing,
hangs in the air above him.
His ears, pink with wind,
the steel ridges of the truck bed
stripe his jeans with cold.
The sleeping dog rides in the back with him.
He can hear his father & two uncles
in the cab laughing. Their heads bob
between the guns on the rack.

On some of the geese the eyes are open.
A nonliving eye not quite clear,
like the clouded face of a watch.
He thinks of flying, how it would feel
to have nothing surround you.

You can hear their call
long before you see them.
He remembers hearing a flock
on another morning. Geese
stitched across the gray cloth of sky
just before the sun rose
red over the uneven mountains.

The birds flying over a boy's sleep,
distant voices lifting up memories —
that distant call
made him want to be good.

The truck rattling over a cattle guard startles
the boy alert & he hears a moan.
At first he thinks it's the dog,
dreaming after birds.
But then another drone releases
from one of the geese.
He had watched them fall, spin around
& crumple, like a kite in a dive,
dying in midair.

He sorts through the bodies,
black heads, pliant collared necks,
plush silvered breasts piled
limp & ruffled. He finds the goose
& holds it, unfolds the shut wings.
In the soft rush
of riffled feathers he feels
the clotted blood where shot entered.

Opening the black visors of the bill,
he covers the nose holes with his fingers
& blows a few breaths of air
into the silty hollow of the bird.

And the dead bird gives back
the boy's own breath
in distinct syllables, nasal & conversational,
before the bill goes slack.
Then the boy breathes harder into the goose,
cradles it and listens

until there is music, a swell of air
returned over the bird's vocal chords, a purr,
a dirge, a lost-soul quaver.
A blue cone of sound, human-made,
or made human.

What I Believed

Today I brought home a rock
found on the Lake Tahoe shore.
The water has worn
into the rock a face.

I hold it in my hand and think back
to what I believed in my youth:
if I skipped a stone
across the skin of the lake
the stone would sing the shape of wind
    and water.

And if late at night
I stood under the wandering light of stars
beneath a certain second-story window
near Dayton, Nevada, and took a pebble
and tossed it up and let it click
against the dark glass, the face of a girl
would appear in the black square above.

She'd come out to me and we'd cross the field
through the sweet reek of wet hay
to the neighbor's barn where the horses
were restless with our presence.
It was there that I came to regard
sex as a large, nervous animal.

The girl's father didn't understand
how the flowers were wrecked
beneath his daughter's window,
the broken tiger lilies I'd stepped on.
Afterwards, we laughed that he was so upset,
but maybe those bright lilies
stood for something he believed in.

In the barn, when I lit the votive candle
I'd brought to light the musky dark,
we saw the powder on my jeans,
vivid-orange where my thighs had brushed
the pollen-laden stems of the taller flowers.
Later, I thought the shape of shadows
trembled with the pitch of our excitement.

In the twisting light of candleflame,
she read the smooth skin
of my face with her fingers.
I wouldn't guess
what time could do.
I think I thought I was already
who I was going to be.
Not knowing yet
that the years would shape, change,
and reveal me.

Aperture

From behind the screen door I watch the cat
in the bunchgrass stalking at dusk.
With the pure attention of religion,
he waits for the skitter of a field mouse,
shiver in an owl's dream.

The cat delivers his limp prey
to the chipped gray paint of the porch.
I step outside, not knowing
if I will punish the cat
or accept the mouse.

At the edge of the porch I kneel and see
the map of red capillaries
in the delicate mouse ear.

I lift it by the tail to toss,
but in the blink of a smug cat's eye
I feel a tug — an escape
back into life.

In the African journals, Livingston tells
of the charging lion that knocked him down.
When he was held in the lion's mouth,
the human body's trance-like response
was to go limp in an ecstatic giving up
that saved. To assume death

to stay alive.

A Confederate soldier at Antietam
played dead when his battalion was overrun.
For a moment he thought he was safe,
but to make sure, the Union infantryman
drove a bayonet into each body on the ground.

When I pick up the mouse
and it jerks from terror-induced sleep,
I feel all that fear
in a small heartbeat.

My panicked fingers let go
and the mouse slips into the brush where it may be
safe for awhile. Though the cat
is all tension now and ready
to pounce again. I shut him in the house,

stand on the porch and watch the first stars
burn holes in the sky.
The dark enlarging around me,
the pupil in a cat's eye.

Ed McClanahan

Harry at the Breach

Way out there at the far edge of the country, just off the campus of Arbuckle State College of Education in Arbuckle, Oregon, that most anonymous of towns, Assistant Professor of History Harrison B. Eastep, M.A., had once, in a previous existence, lived a largely anonymous life in an anonymous apartment at an anonymous address, toiling by day deep in the bowels of Lower Division Humanities at Arbuckle State (there was no Upper Division), holing up at night in his apartment to grade papers and drink blended whiskey and smoke dope and listen to his increasingly unfashionable "progressive" jazz albums, while contemplating The Meaning of It All.

His second marriage had by now — let's say midwinter of 1974 — been dead almost six years, or about twice as long as it had lived. "("You know what I think, Harry?" his wife, Joellen, had said tearfully on her way out. "I think you're just *hiding* behind all that cheap cynicism! You're just scared, Harry!" *Cheap?* he'd asked himself when she and the boy were gone. *If it's so fucking cheap, how come it's costing me so much?*)

For the last couple of years he'd been carrying on a half-hearted affair with a woman named Marcella, a divorced librarian at the state university in Eugene, sixty miles away, but neither of them was enjoying it much (in large part because Marcella's three teenage daughters persisted in treating Harry like The Degenerate Who Came to Dinner), so Harry only saw her every couple of weeks or so, when the sexual imperative asserted its insistent self. Between times, blended whiskey (along with immense nightly cloudbanks of marijuana smoke) provided all the solace he could handle.

Joellen had been right, actually: Cynicism did come cheap in Arbuckle, whose residents took great civic pride in the fact that they lived in the seat of the only county west of the Mississippi River to support Alf Landon for president in 1936.

Fort Leonard Wood, Missouri, where, as a clerk-typist in the U.S. Army, Harry had spent two dismal years mindlessly typing requisitions for laundry soap and toilet paper, remains the only public facility in his experience that could rival Arbuckle State for pure ugliness. The institution had begun life as a teacher's college, but over the years its mission had gradually expanded to include agriculture, engineering, home economics, nursing, accounting and a host of similarly romantic disciplines, with the result that the campus itself was a preposterous confusion of uniformly unimaginative yet utterly contradictory architectural styles.

The stateliest buildings were the ones that made up the original campus, a cluster of eight or nine low, homely but serviceable crenellated red-brick farewell salutes to the Industrial Revolution. They were closely surrounded by several nice stands of elms and maples; in the spring the trees became leafy ambuscades for great raucous flocks of grackles and grosbeaks that unloaded their sodden ballast only when Humanities faculty happened along the sidewalks below. One learned not to mind it much; in Oregon it was always raining something or other anyhow.

But looming over this bucolic little patch of relative serenity was a farrago of towering slabs of steel and glass and concrete, thrusting themselves skyward as if to blot out the very sun itself (on those rare occasions when it endeavored to shine on this gloomy Joe Bltsplk of a campus), each of them — like the new Food Technology building, which the student newspaper proudly dubbed "the largest erection on the Arbuckle campus" — as impersonal and heartless as . . . well, as the largest erection on the Arbuckle campus.

About the feet of these noble piles crept, kudzu-like, an impenetrable maze of interconnected one-story frame barracks, olive-drab relics of the Navy's wartime V-12 officer-training program. Here, in shabby oblivion, resided (or was bivouacked) Lower Division Humanities, including the Departments of Art, Languages and Literature, Social Studies, Band (not Music), and History, an Aegean stable where Harry and his friend and colleague Gil Burgin shared a stall and plied their inglorious trade.

Humanities was a two-year "Service Division," ranking just above Maintenance and Janitorial. Its minions were regarded by the larger Arbuckle faculty much like the famous red-headed stepchild at the family reunion: Assistant Professors of Poultry Management looked down their beaks upon Western Civ instructors as if at indigestible insects; football coaches treated the poor devils who labored in the freshman composition line like something they'd stepped in by mistake. A distinguished Professor of Sanitary Engineering once openly referred in the faculty senate to required humanities courses as "a damned nuisance," and further denounced these la-te-da garnishments to a liberal education — in a soaring flight of rhetoric such as was rarely heard in that august chamber — as "frills, fluff, and frippery!" Students who evinced an unwholesome interest in the humanities were sent packing after their sophomore year, before the condition became contagious.

When Harry first came to Arbuckle, he'd supposed that he was under some personal or moral or even intellectual obligation to do his best to teach a little something, so he included an essay question in his first exam: He asked his students to discuss briefly some of the influences of the Great Plague of London on the religious climate of the time. The first paper he read began, "In this modren world of ours today, our modren medical science . . ." The second paper began, "Daniel Webster, in his dictionary, defines 'influence' as . . ." The third, "In his dictionary, Daniel Webster defines 'climate' as . . ." Harry round-filed the whole batch of papers then and there and began immediately to make out another test, multiple-choice questions only ("The Great Plague was spread by: a. dirty doorknobs, b. old paper money, c. rats, d. illicit sexual intercourse"). Later, he discovered that true-false questions ("Sir Walter Raleigh caught the Great Plague from an Indian maiden in America and brought it home to London with him. T or F?") were even less bothersome to mark, and nowadays he relied on them to the exclusion of all other forms.

So it came to pass that Harry's dedication to pedagogy had eventually eroded to such an extent that when his mother first hinted, in a letter, that he might want to consider coming home to Needmore and going into the antiques racket with her, he found himself, he confided to his officemate Gil Burgin, seriously entertaining the possibility.

"What?" cried Gil, as he scurried off to knock down yet another Western Civ Section. "And give up the Life of the Mind?"

Karen Joy Fowler

For Kevin Collins

"This Child Could Be
Yours." A poster fading behind
glass at McDonald's and my son,
startled, asks, *Is it a contest?*
Is the child a prize? Spaced
teeth, small, definite freckles.
Anyone would want this child.
We order french-fries, a shake
in a waxed cup with a lid,
a hamburger with everything
scraped off, beside the poster
where my son blows the paper
wrapping from his straw onto
the floor and I retrieve it,
fold it. I put it in my pocket
and if I wanted I could
keep it there forever.

Demian Entrekin

The Bright Night

The bright night has fallen and cracked open.
In the crowded desert, my dreams of you come out.
The love you hide has stained me to the bone.

Where summer's eyes have held you for a time
The stars are hidden in dusty curtains of light.
The bright night has fallen and cracked open.

You step and twirl and pivot with a gleam
In the dusty desert. My dreams of you fall out.
The love you hide has stained me to the bone.

We came along to listen for what may seem
To run between us — the rhythm in the beat.
The hot night has fallen and cracked open.

You swim and twirl and listen to a dream
Where summer's eye has held you in its heat.
The love you hide has stained me to the bone.

Where I go from here will never be the same
Though I'll refuse to show what I might.
The bright night has fallen and cracked open.
The love you hide has stained me to the bone.

Thomas Kellar

Primer Gray

Smoke ring in a windstorm.
Old man with blindfold and cigarette.
At the university he showed promise,
was called a diamond in the rough
but the years got away from him.
He pissed away his time.
Now he waits for the phone to ring,
for Gabriel to call
and ask for his last request.

From the beginning
desire was a map without names
never sure where he was
or where he was going.
Change made for the sake of change.
Point A to point B
in a car painted primer gray.
He drank too much
slept too much
read too much
chased easy too much
never finished the novel
he sporadically worked
for 17 years.

Now the Rambler sits on blocks,
the manuscript lost in the basement.
He calls himself "invisible man on blue planet,"
the events of his life written in disappearing ink.
Nothing to offer as evidence
of having circled the sun.
Staring through kitchen window at winter sky
he chain-smokes, sips hot tea,
waits for the angels to raise their rifles
and take him home.

Sands Hall

Chaos Excerpt #1

One morning, Michael and Sara breakfasted at The Stoneground, a bakery in town, and Michael broke a plastic knife while buttering his cinnamon roll. He was outraged by the report of a recent Supreme Court decision and as he talked, loudly, angrily, Sara was aware of the discomfort of the people around them, aware, too, that Michael was smearing unhealthy amounts of butter onto his roll. When his knife snapped the top flew halfway across the room and, with butter still clinging to it, stuck to the cuff of a young man's jeans. Michael stepped over to apologize and explain. His voice carried around the small breakfast area, but the young man was very polite, agreeing with Michael absolutely about the state of the nation.

Eventually the man turned back to his coffee and croissant and Michael sat back down. Sara leaned across the table. "Maybe you shouldn't upset the quiet morning-time of other people, Michael," she whispered.

He looked at her in shock, folded up the newspaper, and left the bakery.

Sara couldn't get hold of him all day. When she did she thought they'd never work through the argument: "Why shouldn't people be bothered at their goddamn breakfasts when the country is going to *hell?*" Michael stormed around the living room, pausing to look at Sara's ficus tree. "This plant has mites or something, look at those brown spots," he said. "The country is going to hell precisely *because* no one wants to be 'disturbed'! Everyone wants to pretend nothing's happening. Well, it *is* happening, and ignoring it isn't going to make it go away. If something I say should just *happen* to make them think, what in *hell* is wrong with that?"

"Michael," Sara sighed, "it's like America's your best friend or something and you're furious at him for lousing up his life."

Michael looked at her with a subdued and grumpy respect. "Her," he said, "I'm furious with her." He pinched a scrolled yellow leaf off the ficus plant. "Try wiping milk on these leaves, or wash them with detergent, something." He crumpled the leaf, looked down at the mosaic of brown bits on his palm. "She's making bad, rotten choices. Why *wouldn't* that piss me off, it should piss everyone off. She throws her money away on stupid, useless things, she's destroying herself, lying to herself, doping up, tarting around, forgetting what it was made her great in the first place, this grand experiment we were supposed to keep *alive*. If we don't stay outraged, Sary, it'll go on this way, you know, and we'll *lose* her." His voice broke. He turned away.

When he would let her, Sara put her arms around him. She saw his point, as she always does. She couldn't help but feel, nevertheless, that people should be allowed to eat their muffins in peace. Mornings can be so difficult.

This difference in their viewpoints keeps them on a somewhat uneven keel: Sara feels guilty and simpleminded; Michael, she is sure, just gets mad when he thinks about it.

Knowing this, and even knowing that his heart is still entangled elsewhere — with the wife from whom he's been separated only a year, and the daughter who lays blood claim to him — even knowing that he will probably return to them, she cannot bring herself to leave him. She wants to lean the pillars of her life up against his. This, she is certain, would make them stronger together than apart. They often have tea in the morning and then as soon as they go their separate ways, there is a moment of panic — they shared this with one another — when they think: But what am I supposed to do now? Without him, without her, at my side? It is odd, scary, uncomfortable; not, as it might sound, romantic.

Mostly, Michael sleeps at Sara's. They have clung to one another through the long nights of two Sierra winters, when the wind snuffles around the house like a hungry hound, scratching and wailing at the cracks to be let in. Perhaps they hold on more out of a need for ballast than out of love. He is the spar and she a drowning woman; or she is the flotsam around which his tired arms can wrap and cling. She accepts that this may be over any minute and is aware that the potential loss of him hovers like an impending death, making the time they have together all the more precious. Their bodies fit together each night like spoons in a velvet casing.

One morning, recently, Sara woke before Michael, and lay content. The weight of his arm over her shoulder and across her chest made her feel contained; one of his hands clasped one of hers. Then she felt him come awake and his breath against the back of her neck was a sigh of such despair that she said, urgently, "What?"

"Ah, Sary." He sounded old and sad.

"What?" Sara said, and she felt her insides go stiff. She swallowed. "Sweetheart, what?"

"I just don't think we're going to make it."

Sara said nothing. Her body had just turned into granite; her heart pumped blood uselessly against a hard exterior wall.

"I just don't see how on earth we're going to make it."

This is it, then, Sara thought. She had been expecting it for weeks, however, months, even, and so she tried to keep her breath flowing. She wondered if on this, their last morning, they would make love, if he would in any case stay for tea, if he would give her time to make the corn muffins that he likes. But she did not move to start any of those things. She thought that if they drifted back to sleep they could pretend the subject had not been broached and they could go on in the transitory, impermanent way to which they have somehow accustomed themselves.

Michael breathed again, another desperate sigh. "What if it's eight years of Bush," he said. "How will we ever make it?"

Sara turned into him with such suddenness that she barked her knee against his and he swore. He couldn't know why she loved him so hard that morning; why she sat on his lap and tugged at the roots of his hair the way he likes while they waited for muffins to bake; why she laughed at everything he said, when outside the rain was misting the pines and the leafless bushes and the houses across the street, making the landscape grey and dreary, depressing.

"You're cheerful this morning," Michael said, and Sara could feel him cheering up himself. "I don't know why, when everything in this nation is going to hell in a handbasket."

Chaos Excerpt #2

Morgan, visiting his brother and sister-in-law in Sierra City, offers to take his 16-month-old nephew, Nat, for a walk. "Just up to Diamond Crossing," he says to his brother, who is helping him strap Nat into the blue canvas and aluminum backpack.

"Bit far," Hyde says.

"It's half a mile, at the most. Isn't it?"

Hyde shrugs. "With Nat, I mean."

"We'll get there," Morgan says. "I need the exercise."

Nat says, "Wak?" With an earnest face which for some reason makes Morgan sad, he tries to help his father manipulate his tiny feet into the leg-holes. Settled, he grins up at Morgan. "Wak!"

With Nat on his back Morgan climbs up the hill back of the house, turning before the trees begin to wave back at Diana, who is watching them go. "See you soon," her high voice floats to them. "Have fun." In her long skirt and work boots — she and Hyde are fixing the antiquated plumbing beneath the bathroom — she looks like a pioneer woman and Morgan feels sad again. His brother is younger and is the one with the wife and the land and the child. He, Morgan, has had one unsuccessful marriage. He does have the nice car that got him here, not paid for yet, and a job to which he needs to return in a few days' time.

"Tree," Nat says, and Morgan agrees with him that yes, it is a tree. "Sky," Nat says, shifting in the backpack as he points up at the patches of blue visible above and between the thick branches above them. Again Morgan agrees that it is the sky.

This point-and-name game had gone on all last night, before, during and after dinner, while his brother glowed with subdued pride at the number of words Nat knows. Morgan has no way of assessing if Nat's acquisition of language is normal or if he does indeed have the superior intelligence his parents assume.

He is quickly out of breath. Thirty-five pounds of child on his back is far more of a weight than he had expected, and at first the path takes them almost directly up the hill, no switchbacks. He stops to pant. "Out of breath," he says to Nat. "But never fear. We'll get there."

Nat points again, saying something that Morgan does not understand. He mimics the sound, though, as if he is agreeing, and places one boot in front of the other on the path, watching the scuffed toes come and go beneath him. He wants a child of his own but is also aware, watching Diana and Hyde with Nat, that he might not be able to bear the time and effort it seems to demand. And in any case, there is no woman in his life. Still, if he waits much longer he will truly be too old: he doesn't want to be dealing with PTA meetings when he's forty-seven, with a teenager's acne when he's fifty-four.

Morgan reflects on the amount of anxiety he's caused his own parents, long past the years when he might have expected that to be the case. His mother had told him, when he'd cracked up his car and was still in the hospital recovering, that it never got any better for her, either. "It's as hard to watch you now, Morgan, or the grief you went through when Rebecca decided to leave you, as it was to watch your agony when dear old Homer got run over, or even that time you scraped your knee so badly falling off your tricycle."

She wasn't crying, but she wiped at her eyes with the back of a hand that was wrinkled, spotted with something larger than freckles but as brown. "You never stop wanting to console, to do something to comfort," she said. "In a way it's even worse, now that you and Hyde are older, because there's less I'm allowed to do. Less I can do. It used to be hugging you was enough. To make the pain go away."

She had been holding his hand, and he had turned his head to look at the patient sleeping in the bed beside him; he didn't want her to see the tears in his own eyes. He wished a hug from his mother would take the pain in his shoulder and hip away, wished she could make it all better, the insurance hassles, the wrecked car, the memory of the crash he relived over and over every night until he thought he would go out of his mind from trying to think how he could have made it through the moment differently. He envied Nat. Last night his nephew had wept inconsolably when the dog barked at him. "He's just tired," Diana had said, scooping him up, cuddling him. "You're just tired, aren't you, little one." She pulled up her shirt and gave him a breast. Nat's sobs had died to an occasional hiccup as he nursed, a tiny hand kneading the swell of Diana's white flesh. Morgan had turned his eyes away, afraid, embarrassed, that Diana or Hyde might see the longing there.

Nat begins to squirm in the backpack. "Down," he says.

"No, Nattie. We've got to keep going if we're going to get to our destination."

"Desnation," Nat tries, but then says, again, "Down!"

Morgan stops, lets the pack slip off his shoulders, unsnaps the buckles and straps, and lifts Nat free. Nat takes his hand and leads the way up the path, although in order to keep hold of his fist Morgan has to stoop a little. His boots fall silently on the piles of gold and red leaves and he breathes deep of a smell that is unfamiliar to him — he's been brought up in Southern California and visits Hyde less than he would like — but which is pleasant: leaves and pine and something that hits the back of his throat and makes him think of snow.

Nat stops and squats, examining something on the path. "That's a stick," Morgan says.

"Tick," Nat repeats.

Morgan takes his hand again, saying, "We gotta move it, buddy," but Nat continues to squat, examining stick after stick — small branches, really, slimmer than a pencil — and saying "Tick, tick." After a few moments of this Morgan picks Nat up, hoisting him onto one hip. But Nat squirms and kicks, wanting to stay where he is.

"Come on, Nattie." Morgan tries to pick him up again. "We've got quite a way to go yet."

But Nat shakes his head and says, "No!" When Morgan insists on carrying him he screws his face up, saying words that Morgan doesn't understand, and begins to cry.

'Oh, brother." Morgan puts him down. "How the hell are we going to get there if you act like this, huh?"

Nat stops crying. Morgan stares down at the tousled blonde head, so like his own, which is bent over a pile of leaves. He puts his hands on his hips, staring up the winding path that disappears into a group of trees. The leaves are brilliant yellow. Twined around the trunks are plants whose leaves are crimson; the two colors, together, make him think about painting, although he is not an artist. He wishes he could capture it. "Come on," he says again, but when Nat doesn't respond, squats beside him.

Nat digs his stick into the ground until it breaks, which makes him laugh. In spite of himself, Morgan smiles. Nat finds another stick and digs its point into the ground until this one, too, snaps and again he chortles with glee. Morgan laughs too and allows himself to settle onto the path. He tucks a foot beneath him and balances mostly on the boot and ankle so that the back of his pants don't get completely wet. He stares down the path of trodden leaves which snakes down the hill and out of sight, into another grove. He wonders if Hyde knows the names of all the trees around here. Probably. Hyde knows how to chop wood

and owns a chain saw, has built much of the house in which he and
Diana live, adding on to the pre-existing shack that came with the
property. Hyde understands engines and knows how to bake bread.
He'd lived alone for a long time before he'd found Diana. They don't
show their affection much, but their love for each other emanates from
them like so much light, or a scent of perfume, and Morgan hates that
observing this, too, would make him sad.

Beside him, Nat bends his knees and with a huge amount of arm
preparation, throws a stick down the path, away from them. "Good
throw!" Morgan says, and picks up a stick and throws it too. Nat claps
his hands and gives Morgan several sticks to throw, thrilled with the
distance his uncle can hurl them. Each time a stick lands farther than
the one before, Nat bends his knees and puts his hands on them,
squinting, as if he's had something to do with the distance the stick has
traveled.

"We should get a move on, buddy," Morgan says, though he stays
where he is. He takes a kind of pleasure in the ache of his ankle,
twisted beneath him, supporting his weight. He hears the call and then
the reply of two birds and tries to spot them in the branches overhead.

Nat brings Morgan a stone he has found. "Rock," he says, laying it
in Morgan's palm. His tiny fingernails are filled with dirt.

"Wow," Morgan says, and examines the minute colorations of the
stone, swirls of grey and white inside the black. "Wow," he says again,
meaning it this time.

Nat turns around and in a movement which Morgan observed the
night before, when Nat wanted Diana to read to him, squirms his
diapered rear end onto Morgan's lap. He sits as if Morgan is his throne,
his hands placed majestically on either of Morgan's thighs. Together
they survey the forest and field that fall away beneath them. Morgan
rests his chin on Nat's head, and with each breath feels his stomach
touching Nat's back.

He realizes that their breath is moving in and out at the same time
but as soon as he observes this it changes, and Nat slides off his lap.
"Want to go home?" Morgan asks, standing, and Nat puts his hands up.

Descending, Nat on one hip, and the pack over a shoulder, Morgan is
amazed how little distance they have traveled from the cabin. But Diana
says, "You were gone a nice long time. Did you have fun, Nattie?"

Morgan gives her the black stone. "Nat wants you to have this," he
says.

Nat points at it. "Rock."

Diana's eyes gleam. "Why, thank you, Nattie!" She swoops down and kisses his cheek. "And thank you, Morgan, for taking him. It was great to get some work done around here." She rises up on tiptoe to kiss Morgan's cheek. "Thank you."

Hyde comes in, carrying a step ladder, and lugs it to the door of the bathroom. He stands there, shaking his head. "What a mess."

"You get going on the plumbing," Diana says, "and then discover what's weird about the electricity."

"Whoever built this place had a wild sense of logic," Hyde says. "How was Diamond Crossing?"

Morgan watches Nat wander toward his toys, piled beneath the crib. "We didn't exactly get there."

Jane Hirshfield

Clock

There is no substance
that does not carry one inside it,
hands spinning
as the Fates were said to do.

Or, more truly, carry many:
in one body the clock of the knee
and the ankle-clock keep different times,
the swaying metronome of the breast ignores
the solstice curve of rib that supports it.

Nor does the body's clock
govern its soul's,
which may move more quickly or slower —
a divergence seen in some moods
as tragic, comic in others.

All clocks in themselves are serene.
It is their task to run down.

And so the clock of the tree
welcomes its beetles and lichens,
the clock of the house feasts with its termites.

And still the clock of the marrow
spills out its cells gone wrong
and the clock of the family falters, unoiled and forgotten.
The living clock of fallible springs runs
side by side with the death-clock of quartz,
and neither clock can touch the hands of the other.

Some clocks are indifferent and perfect,
others bend over as walking animals under strong wind.

Even the clock of blue, uprisen granite
carries within it
the cooling clock of its own erosion to gruss.
Whole ranges this way disappear, obeying their clocks,
while the clock of a grove of aspen,
in theory immortal,
still shivers each season's gold-leaf into the wind.

A wet dog comes into the kitchen to shake off her wetness.
The drops fall, then dry: a clock's ticking gone suddenly still.

The clock of a memory
not remembered is not stopped,
as the clock of a memory remembered is not stopped.

Neither do these clocks grow larger or smaller,
greater or lesser, more bitter or sweet.
They stay on their walls, their dashboards, their wrists.
There, they are called watches, as if observers,
as if that close to the body they could look back.

Clock of the bamboo dipper that fills with water
then clacks itself empty, unlistened to, year after year;
gravity egg-clock of turned-over three-minute sand;
clock of the isotope's half-life, of a spotted mare come into heat;
star-clocks of Stonehenge, of Chichen Itza,
of the rotating earth-face that holds two numbers only, light and then dark.
Clock of a pickup's engine leaking its oil,
"Three weeks before she needs some, steady as clockwork."

They do not look back.
They do not look, concerned with neither our terror nor joy.
Only the eye looks at them,
looks and looks while swimming its river of lubricant tears —
some shuddered in unconcealed loudness;
some whispered silent over the cheekbones and down the chin's crevice;
most — steady slipstream of life still living — held for all time.

The merest glimmer, blinked back almost unnoticed,
as the blinking of a watchface goes almost unnoticed, until it is gone.

Laressa Dickey

Ave Maria

There is no place to lay my grandmother's bones.
In fact, there are no bones.

Maria died and left her silver and black rosary,
her spools of thread, a freezer stocked with Lucky Strikes.
She left Christmas presents in red tree paper,
worn books smelling of cigarettes.
She left no one her recipe for spaghetti.

She left her TV tuned to the baseball game,
left tomato soup and buttered crackers.
Her "Bless us O Lord for these thy gifts
which we are about to receive from thy bounty, amen."
She left her crucifix, her Hail Marys.
She left her door locked.

She left some medical student her blackened lungs,
her nearly ruptured aneurysm, swollen ankles.
Sore-covered face. She left them
her Rh negative factor and her delicate hands.

She left me a moth-eaten book of poetry,
her Royal typewriter and Chesterton's "Donkey."
Maria died, and left me hungry.

W. Scott McLean

A Letter to My Grandfather

for Rudolph Wilfred Wallin, in memoriam
& for Ed Vaughn

Dear Grandpa,

There is no one in this world I can write, only you where I sat tonight,
stroking the neck of the young deer I'd hit on the North Bloomfield
Road driving home. The buck rushed out from behind a big cedar at a
bend in the road, more like a rabbit than a deer, right under the wheels
of the truck. When I turned around he'd crawled off to the side of the
road, sitting on his belly legs all busted apart, gasping, I dragged him off
the pavement, asking his forgiveness talking & crying the whole time. I
can't remember how I came to get him into the woods & downslope,
throwing branches downhill I laid him up in a bed of oak leaves, & sat
with him, the deep brown eyes staring off into space stroking the fur of
his neck, desperately wanting his pain to end.

How unprepared I came to this. I took out a knife thinking I could end
his misery only to know I could not kill surely, quickly, with the
absolute certainty & skill demanded & I would only compound the
grief. So I got back in the truck & headed home to get the 22, but
knew halfway there that was little better, & drove up to Ed's house. He
stood for a minute in the hall as I told him about the deer & then
moved back upstairs with a solemnity I felt in my whole body. We got
out a 9mm revolver, loaded it.

I sat for one brief moment again with the buck, asked for three bless-
ings on him, that his path into whatever world be without the pain &
misery of his lying there. Ed put the 9mm to his head, all I saw was the
orange-red flash, & felt the sound all through the woods. I knelt down
& stroked the buck again, prayed he be out of his pain, but there was
no bullet hole I could see, his eyes glazed over & clouded by bits of dirt.
The eye-blink gone, we fired a second shot to the head to make sure

we had done what we needed. I made another small bow, & we drove home.

You remember, all those antlers you had in your garages, in northern Minnesota, then in San Clemente & Seal Beach where you first showed me how to work with tools. The dates you had taken the deer were painted in red on aluminum you'd brushed over the skull bases. It was what I always first saw when I came into the garage, & I remember still the stories about how you fed Mom & the whole family during the depression by hunting deer in the Minnesota woods. Years later the first time Dad met you he told me was in your basement where you were dressing out a deer. I always admired your abilities, to do what needed to be done. And now, I don't have those skills, to do what needs to be done here. I couldn't take him home, dress him out, though Chuck once told me, "It's not hard, Scott, especially all the fish you've cleaned, they're just bigger & look like us on the inside."

These deer pass through our lives every day, I greet them in the orchard & am happy they take the apples & pears on the lower branches, & whatever falls on the ground. Evenings below the house they gather in the kidkitdizze where I throw rotten fruit for them; I talk with them but they move silently away. They are bound to us as we to them, whole families of deer moving in our lives where people used to hunt them, kill, in gratitude & recognition, in loving kindness for the life given, that much I am sure of. Where I sat tonight, in a dark night of life & death, trying to comfort the deer but with little real comfort in it, unable to take the gift, I went downslope with my neighbor, able only to end the pain but not silence the grief & the sadness.

Gary Snyder

What to Tell, Still

Reading the galley pages of Laughlin's *Collected Poems*
with an eye to writing a comment,
how warmly J. speaks of Pound,
    I think back to —

At twenty-three I sat in a lookout cabin in gray whipping wind
at the north end of the northern Cascades,
high above rocks and ice, wondering
    if I should go visit Pound at St. Elizabeth's.

And studied Chinese in Berkeley, went to Japan, instead.

J. puts his love for women
his love for love, his devotion, his pain, his causing-of-pain,
    right out there.

I'm 63 now, & I'm on my way to pick up my ten-year-old stepdaughter
    and drive the car pool;
I just finished a five-page letter to the County Supervisors   dealing with a
former supervisor,
    now a paid lobbyist,
who has twisted the facts, and gets paid for his lies. Do I
have to deal with this creep? I do.

James Laughlin's manuscript sitting on my desk.
Late last night reading his clear poems —
and Burt Watson's volume of translations of Su Shih,
    next in line for a comment on the back.

September heat.
The Watershed Institute meets,
      planning more work with the B.L.M.
And we have visitors from China, Forestry guys,
      who want to see how us locals are doing with our plan.
Editorials in the paper are against us,
      a botanist is looking at the rare plants in the marsh.

I think of how J. writes stories of his lovers in his poems —
      puts in a lot,
      it touches me.

So recklessly bold — foolish — ?
to write so much about your lovers
when you're a long-time married man. Then I think,
what do I know?
      About what to say
      or not to say, what to tell, or not, to whom,
      or when,

      still.

Winter

Bruce Hawkins

To Conjure With

Sound of ping pong in a garage at dusk,
rapid rallies of fairly competent players,
moths in lampshades rattling pizzicato,
a pack of Camels opening,
the string quartets of yesterday's chili.

A sack of potato chips crackles
and a dog's nails scrabble on linoleum;
bed springs and frogs tell their stories.

Something at midnight slips into a pond
destroyed by the crass directionless roar.
Rumplestiltskin is working. You can hear him.
The morning paper thwacks against the door.

Tires on the late night street
and bacon cooking are the same swift rush.

Every sound escapes into another;
all sound scurries from this world.

Those mice behind the wall,
the indescribably small srritch of the light string
turning the room into something I can recognize.

I can look at the stars and know
they shine because they are stuffed
with the background noise of all our lives.
Think of a sound year, the long grinding climb,
a nose blown after hours of sobbing.

We drove through a low place
and mayflies, mating in midair,
turned our windshield into soup.
Silence is always as brief as their flight.
Back and forth our wipers labored, whispering,
in immediate response,
the way you can't help blurting out
some stupid thing. Anything! Just anything!

.

The Woodcutter's Cabin

The stubble field is vast,
a shaven mound growing back after the baby.
It stretches to the dark line of trees.
Field mice, garter snakes, pheasants, quail —
the earth streams with what it hides.

The hunters follow the forest's edge,
their dogs relaxed and chasing each other now,
their guns unloaded. They negotiate
the last fence, leaning their twelve gauges on the posts,
holding the wires apart to climb through.
From here they can make out the windows
grown calm as green melons in the dusk.

Giving back the heat of the day
the ground has a baked and easy sense.
As they approach, the chimney
lets go a careful scribble of smoke
above the black pine-snaggled rise,
and a full moon, which has been lurking
faint as a talcumed ghost

in the sky all afternoon, cries out
with a new minted gleam
while at their backs, crouched in shadows,
a pheasant answers, one biting laugh
that scoots and bristles in their scalps.

Leaving a Small Town on Foot at Dawn

Iron rings above garage doors
stand fishing in air.
The nets, when there are nets,
have no bottoms.

I leave a string of perfect feet
across the frosted lawn.
A splash of egg yolk
seeps through a crack on the horizon.

The nets behind me continue to catch nothing.
It's what they were made for.
It's why they've waited all these years.

I walk down the middle of the road now,
breaking the ice on puddles.
The smoke stands thick as sweatsocks in the chimneys.

Bruce Hawkins

All Summer the Silence

All summer the silence has been
a green, dripping sullenness of conquered things
and now music climbs in the trees . . .
relief, release
                        of leaves.

For years I have moved against my nature,
the soothing underside of fire,
the too obvious fountains within the crust of bark,
the oneness of logs in a fireplace long after midnight
and the sizzle of rain on a roof.

For years the trees refused to speak.
I watch an old man raking fire from his yard.
He comes too close to my flame wrinkled mind
and makes me need to spit my image at him.

His old face is a stiff
extension of his brain;
I watch the lone thought playing there,
the furtive child who feels
his whole existence captured in a jar,
still trying to hide above the grey eyebrows:
"I'll rake death out of my life,
 I'll rake it away, I'll rake it away.
 I'll sweep my sidewalk clean."

I wander among these remnants of forests,
these captives in parking strips
all mutilated and cut low for phone wires.
They refuse to speak
but they can't stop the music from climbing in them.
They can't stop the music
                              or the messages
each twisting free
                    riding brightly on a breeze

the counterparts of weeping long withheld
in public rooms where air is portioned out
and slides to us through tubes.

Forrest Hamer

A Month of Sundays

The first Sunday after the Sunday you were buried,
we talked almost forever, walking together
toward home, in the middle of a long road.

The next Sunday after, we'd fought, and I had to return
to California, and we were saying goodbye, saying
*people who love each other sometimes get on
each other's nerves*, and *these are small matters*.
We held each other for the long time
we held each other when I left last summer.

The third Sunday after, I woke up not having dreamt,
wanting to call home, knowing Dad would be at church
and the answering machine would pick up, your voice clear
as dream, promising you would call me back.

Jeanne Wakatsuki Houston

A Taste of Snow

I first saw snow one Christmas when I lived in the high desert of Owens Valley, California. I was nine years old. It was during the Second World War, the first winter my family and I spent at Manzanar. When the crystal flakes floated down, like translucent coconut chips dancing in the breeze, I ran out into the clear area between the barracks, twirling and dancing and opening my mouth to catch the powdery ice. The snow reminded me of cotton candy, wispy and delicate, and gone with one whisk of the tongue.

I was surprised by the sharp coldness of the air and somehow disappointed that such beauty had its price to be paid — icy feet and hands, and uncomfortable wetness when the snow melted upon contact with my clothes and face. Still, the utter loveliness of this new phenomenon was so overpowering I soon forgot my discomfort.

Other people began coming out of the barracks into a transformed world. Some carried brightly colored Japanese parasols and wore high wooden *getas* to raise their stockinged feet above the snow. It was odd not to hear the "kata-kata" clatter of wooden clogs scraping across sand and gravel. The blanket of snow muffled sound and thickened the thin planed roofs of the barracks, softening the stark landscape of white on white. It was strangely soothing to me, silent and tranquil. I found myself moved to tears.

This particular imprint in my memory is easily explained. Before being sent to Manzanar we lived in Ocean Park, on Dudley Avenue, a block from the beach. Ocean Park Pier was my playground. All the kids in the neighborhood played ball and skated along the wide cement promenade that bordered the beach from Ocean Park to Venice.

Memories of Ocean Park are warm ones of sunshine, hot days on the beach, building sand castles, playing *Tarzan* and *Jungle Girl*, jumping off lifeguard stands and spraining ankles. Fourth of July was a balmy evening of crowds milling around the pier waiting for fireworks to spray the sky with luminous explosives. Easter was as colorful as the many-hued eggs the local service club buried in the sand for the kids to uncover. And Christmas was just another version of this type of buoyant, high-spirited celebration my family enjoyed before the war.

In my memory Christmas morning seemed always sunny and clear. Strolling along the promenade in my new orange-flowered dress and white high-topped shoes, pushing the doll carriage Santa had left under the big tree in our living room, I proudly displayed myself and my gifts as did the other children of the neighborhood. My oldest brother Bill, who was then in his twenties, walked with me and helped me feed popcorn to the pigeons warbling and pecking around our feet. Then he rushed me off in his old blue roadster to visit his girlfriend Molly, who played the violin while he sang, and I slept.

Like a story within a story, or a memory within a memory, I cannot think of one memorable Christmas, but of these two. They are yin and yang, each necessary to appreciate the other. I don't remember Christmas trees in Manzanar. But we gathered driftwood from the creeks that poured down from the nearby Sierras and across the high desert. With these we improvised. In my mind's eye they co-exist: a lush, brilliantly lit fir tree, and a bare manzanita limb embellished with origami cranes.

To this day, when I travel in the high country, I can cry seeing nature's exquisite winter garb and remembering my first taste of snow.

Marilee Richards

Surviving

'

And so we drove back, slowly,
in a late night rain, the street lights
dappling patterns on your face
staring out into the last remnants
of hope, shoulders slumped
as you swayed in your thoughts.
We had been talking about the distant past
as if by ignoring this freefall
into despair a solution would occur,
wafting gently into place like a wing
with you tucked neatly in its cleft.
We were drinking bourbon from plastic cups
and in the silence that followed
what we had to say I could feel
your shallow breaths disconnecting
and floating like ghosts
into some other life. Never

had you seemed so fatigued,
your grief so permanent, so impervious
to the voices calling you back.
The streets were gushing down torrents
tinged with the same muddy hue
I once saw during a storm
on a thin mountain road. The car
in front had simply washed off
the side. I pulled over
in the downpour as far as I could

and sat, afraid for myself as well,
knowing I could do nothing more
than wait for the weather to spend
itself out and then look
into the canyon lined
with emerging stars to see
if anyone was left alive.

How an Older Man Makes Love

Not as if seeing Jupiter through a telescope
and, holding his breath transfixed, he marvels
at his first heavenly body, orbital
and unclothed. Nor
as a boy who leans out from a train gathering speed
and tries to face the wind, but its strength
tears his eyes and the birds, the flowers
whizzing past are a kaleidoscopic blur. No.
                                    Realizing
timing is everything, an older man polishes
the same smooth stone. The country
of strawberry skin is safe in his patient
hands as his dusty breath shuffles in and out
from the warm nest of his lungs. Each
valley and fold help him remember where
he has been, which faint scent to follow
next, and I have to admire how friendly
shadows collect, slightly wavering, almost ready.
When he is tired he rests, knowing to hurry
is to fail because anywhere
is the same familiar place he has returned to
again and again. Through shutters his cry
exfoliates summer gold from trees.
A blue vein over softening bone —
I kiss his pulse.

Alicia Suskin Ostriker

First Betrayal

Remember back to then.
O we were never behaving children.
We stood and watched as all
The sky came down, like a white wall
Tumbling slowly
Ate apples in the snow
And stood and laughed. How could we know
We hung upon a crust, a dust, this place
A pebble pinned in space?
                    O children, mind,
Infinity has driven angels blind
With whiteness, and they fell
Twisting, tearing their sky-speared eyes; and hell
Was limitless, the demons fall forever
Fall white, cease never.
                    Foolish, we never guessed
Deceit, but always thought the snow was blessed,
As if the earth were solid and had roots,
We stood so steadfast in our shiny boots.

Katherine McCord

Say You Are Me

Give me the
center of your
hand, the chart.
I'm going to
read what
I've done
to you.

———

I'm lying on
my bed in
shoes, jacket, coat;
it's about warmth,
the quest for
love and sleep.
You're not here.
None of you are
here.

———

James D. Houston

Prologue

from The Trail Notes of Patty Reed
Santa Cruz, California
October 1920

Last night I dreamed again about my mother. She was standing in the snow. There were trees with snow-laden branches. She wore a long coat, and her hair hung loose. Her arms reached toward me. She was speaking words I could not hear. I ran through the snow, while her mouth spoke the silent words. I was young, a little girl, and also the age I am now. For a long time I ran toward her with outstretched arms. Finally I was close enough to hear her soft voice say, "You understand that men will always leave you."

I stopped running and in my mind called out to her, "No. It isn't so!"

Her mouth twitched, as if she were about to speak again. She wanted to say, "Listen to me, Patty." She was trying to say it.

I woke up then and spoke aloud. "Women leave you too."

I was speaking right to her, and I waited, expecting to hear her voice in my ear, as if she were close by me in the dark. I whispered, "Don't you remember?"

But she was gone.

I dropped back against my pillow and lay there half the night trying to fall asleep so she would come to me again and speak again. I couldn't sleep. I had started thinking about her life and papa's life and all our lives, about who stays and who leaves who, and when, thinking how a man can be right there next to you and at the same time somehow gone off by himself, or maybe already gone away forever, how a mother can do that too, thinking then about all of them from those years so long ago, walking in and out of my mind like people in a pageant, ordinary people who did not expect such a crowd to be watching them pass by, papa and mama, my brothers and sister, the

teamsters and mule skinners and grizzled husbands on their dried-up
wagon seats and their women watching the trail ahead and the Indians
who traveled with us from time to time, every kind of Indian you can
think of, Sauk and Delaware and Sioux and Shoshone and Paiute and
Washo and Miwok, along with all the others we met by accident on the
way, though when you look back it seems anything but accidental.

Now, this morning, from my porch I watch the road that runs
beside the lagoon and down to the beach. Between the beach and this
lagoon there is a rail line that follows the sand. It's an odd sight.
Hundreds of pilings support the track, like a centipede walking from
town to town along the shoreline. Beyond the sand the water's edge
today is quiet, like a lake. Beyond the beach, beyond the rail line, the
Pacific Ocean spreads and spreads.

When I was a girl there were no trains anywhere yet out here.
When we came through the mountains there was hardly any trail.
Where the train cuts through the Sierra Nevada now, we made that
trail. What a long road we have followed. And it has finally brought me
here, to yet another house, where I have become another old woman
looking out, looking back.

The ocean I see is not what we came searching for. The farthest
border of the land was not our goal, but the land itself. I should say *his*
goal — the farthest land my father could envision, where he would
somehow be his own man at last or be a new man in some new way and
have a hand in starting something fresh and bigger than himself. I am
not saying this is how it turned out. But these were his dreams. He was
a dreamer, as they all were then, dreaming and scheming, never
content, and we were all drawn along in the wagon behind the
dreamer, drawn along in the dusty wake.

When you are eight years old, of course, you worship your father,
as I worshipped mine. We trusted him to get us through these situations no one could have prophesied ahead of time. As long as he was
riding beside the wagon on his precious mare, we figured nothing could
go too far wrong. That's how tall he was in my eyes then.

Seventy years and more go by, and everything looks different. I
look at where the dreaming led papa, and led us, and I cannot excuse
him as I could when I was eight, or eighteen, or even twenty-eight. Yet
neither is it my place to judge him, as others have, or judge the way he
contended with the trials of that crossing. Some have blamed him
entirely and blame him even now, after all this time, since he was the
one who had organized the journey out of Springfield in the first place.

Donner, of course, is the name that stuck, the one they have named
the lake for and the route through the mountains and the monument
that stands beside the route, with its brave-eyed family cast in bronze
atop a pedestal raised as high as the snow that year was deep.

Maybe it has been a blessing, in the end, since the name itself
causes a shroud to fall around the one who utters it, having become a
synonym for disaster, poor planning, and savage behavior that makes
the average person shudder and also salivate for the gruesome details of
what went on. I have read stories and articles of what happened during
that hateful winter until I am sick to death. Newspaper reporters and
photographers still come around here to hound and pester me as if the
only thing I ever did my entire life was spend five months in the snow.
And yet, with all these books and diaries and endless accounts and
semi-truths and outright fantasies that have spread around the world,
the story of our family has been only partly told, and the story of my
father. I have had a hand in that, I admit. Like a good daughter I have
tried through the years to paint him as a hero, even when I knew
better. And I do not apologize one bit. Why should I? He did some
things almost anyone could call heroic. But now that there's only me
and the last few others still alive, there's no harm saying he did other
things that gathered enemies to him like an open jar of jam will gather
ants and blowflies, and this cannot be denied.

You take his wagon — a good example of what I'm talking about.
Did he foresee that it would be the biggest contraption on the western
trail? Did he foresee that his children would be envied and pursued by
others hoping for the chance to ride along and test the springs in the
fancy seats? Did it occur to him that other men would laugh behind his
back, calling it ingenious, but also grandiose, while women would
resent his wife for traveling as if she were some kind of Arabian
princess?

"If they'd have thought of it," I once heard papa say in his own
defense, "they'd all be riding along like this."

It takes you half a lifetime to figure out what your folks were really
up to when you were young. Eventually you come to know them and
what they were capable of. You get to be my age, their very natures lurk
within your own, as year by year more and more of who they were is
revealed to you. Some things I never heard my mother say with her
living voice, I hear her saying now, her voice alive somewhere within
me. Her face visible somewhere in my face. I look in the mirror. I say,
There's mama. There's papa.

Sometimes very early, before it gets light, I will still see him the way he looked the day we left Illinois. In his face I see true pleasure and a boyish gleam that meant his joy of life was running at the full. I see him with his hat tipped back, standing by the wagon he designed himself, the one other travelers would come to call the Palace Car. Everyone else who started West had been content with horses, mules, oxcarts, Conestogas. But not James Frazier Reed. A double-decker Palace Car that took four yoke to pull it, with upholstered seats inside, and a thoroughbred racing mare, and hired hands, and brandy after dinner — that was Papa's vision of being a pioneer. At least, when we started out it was. I have to say this for him, his vision was not like anyone else's I have heard of.

Anita Barrows

The Black Dog

I still feel her dying in me, the black dog
hit by a pickup on a rainy Saturday the winter my life split apart.
Driving the narrow ridge near Bodega, I saw those kids
skid into her & take off. I stopped,
dragged her into the leaves, covered her
with my parka. Rain soaked the dirt. I could hear blood
pool in her throat. For as long as it took — half
an hour? — I held her head in my hands, kept murmuring
There's a good girl, there's a good girl.
Then I felt her relax, the way she might have eased down
into straw-colored grass after a long run. That day I had nothing left
she became what I grieved; I became the world
letting her go.

Claudette Mork Sigg

Mourning on Sandy Bar

Charles F. Hamilton (c. 1823-?)
Postmortem Portrait of Eloise Channing
Quarter Plate Ambrotype, Collection of the Bancroft Library

The daguerreotypist paused, his equipment over his shoulder.
"Let's bring her out into the light," he said to the child's father.

The mother washed the girl's small fingers, studied
a bruise on the right palm, the scratch across sunburned knuckles.
She noted the nail of the right thumb bitten close,
kissed it furtively, paused as if listening.
She was careful about water, so long had she hoarded
each drop that came their way as they crossed the plains.
Nothing wasted, even now, though this evening would see
her daughter buried above a sandy bar of river,
a place without a name where men grubbed in mud and rock,
men whose only condolences were nuggets laid in her palm.

She took her girl's best dress from the trunk,
white silk with cherry ribbons at the shoulders, the sleeves
wide, edged with lace. Lifting her, she slipped arms
into sleeves, letting the child's head rest against her shoulder
as if both were falling asleep at the conclusion of a fairy tale.

They carried the bier outside. A miner standing apart
handed her a small bouquet of lupine and poppies. Taking it,
she paused, swallowed — then bent over the child,
folded small hands over the bright blue and gold flowers.

"You'll be glad you have this," the daguerreotypist said.
She felt her husband nod, saw herself in the years ahead
take out the picture, look at it, touch it.
Turning her face away from the setting sun, she felt darkness
begin to fill the empty spaces around her.

Specimen

Yesterday I excavated my grave.
It was an unintentional discovery,
the site newly carved out of raw red earth,
flint arrowheads, scattering of glass beads,
three bullets, blunted.

The shroud had gone to earth,
the skull fallen from its nest
into a puddle of rainwater.

With hands that trembled, I reached
down into the clear water,
clouded sky reflected above me,
my face in the water.

My face
without flesh or eyes
or scant hair to frame it all,
but mine to hold
between two winter-cold hands,
mine to brush away the peat-scented earth,
mine to label with inked numbers,

> Remembering I had been here . . .

> > running,
> > the crack of thunder in a blue sky,
> > and then, the smell of earth, leaves,
> > the scent of dying things.

Tony D'Arpino

A Rural Pen

A rural pen
Tattoos the goats
Parading up the hill
In dancing goat-file
To the light flashing
In the metal buckets

The dogs are damp
Today the rain melts snow
And the grey stamped ground
Oozing silver ribbons
Becomes a tarnished mirror
Around the pungent stables

The surly neighbors loiter
In the muddy feedlots
Among the cat-like cows
Soon it will be spring
Bare fingers of the orchard
Still prisoners of winter's extra day.

George Keithley

First Morning

Autumn is finished — yesterday in a flash
storm, the worst since my father's death,
then last night's freeze. At once granite
outcrop wears a milky glaze; all
the lean hemlocks are sheathed in ice.
At dawn walking from the meadow
to the woods I wish for the warmth
of his voice. A peaceable man — only
injustice angered him. How might
we meet again if not hiking
in these frosted fields? No hunter,
he loved to discover animals
in their habitat, then leave them
undisturbed. Which he thought just.
"They earn their peace among us.
Let them be." The wren in its nest;
the half-dozen frogs surviving
— who can say how — in a bog-hole;
two owls attracted to the gloom
of the horse barn.
                          His patience will take
years to learn — it's time I start home
to my own children. Emerging
from a stand of pines shagged with cold,
the needles silvered overnight,
I surprise a fox and it bolts
to safety. Bushy tail barely
twitching the ghostly grass or ice-
crusted manzanita, it leaves
little trace. Shafts of sunlight strike
an opaque blue-white sheen which clings
to the county road. It's the first
morning of winter, and the world
is made of glass the heart must break.

Living Again

Then he remembered the blue house where they'd lived.
Her hair nesting on her shoulder as in this photo.
The firm weight of her breast. His hand opened.
The frame struck the floor; glass shattered —

He tore his shirt to reach the pain. Now
he choked on the silence in the cabin.
No breath. The door banged open. He stumbled

through the pines. Into the meadow. Pools of snowmelt among the budding thistles, lupine.
Still he did not cry out. His mouth a mute O.

Above the silver river he saw a hawk flicker.
His chest on fire, he forgot his right hand
full of excuses. Fell among mule-ear. Grass

growing dim. Waking, on his hands and knees,
he noticed the pain that gripped his heart
had eased into his shoulders. Deep

in his belly his breath welled up. Again
the hawk flashed its blood-red tail
in the wind. He rose, slowly. Saw tawny

cattails nodding. Poppies. The first purple
thistles. He listened. For what? When
he was about to die he'd remembered the dark

rain in her voice. Spring rain falling all night
in the Sierra, lifting the river above its bank,
drenching the green meadow, waking sun-gold blossoms.

Then did his heart recover its rhythm, his mind
its balance? He took two steps. Heard water churn;
slosh sedge grass, slap rocks. A chill light

rushed downstream. When he saw it shiver past
the black mudbank, already he'd begun to choose
this life in which our words follow one another
to the end: snowmelt, granite, hawk, poppies, river.

Sierra Songs & Descants

Contributors

Karla Arens is a journalist, poet, and garden writer. She was poetry editor for *Wild Duck Review* and her work has appeared in *Yoga Journal, Earthsave*, and other publications. She has just completed her 33rd winter in the Sierra foothills.

Will Baker is the author of three nonfiction books and four novels, and has had over fifty poems, short stories, articles, and essays published in various literary journals. A teacher at UC Davis for 26 years, he now divides his time between writing and ranching.

Anita Barrows is a poet, translator, essayist, and clinical psychologist. A recipient of many awards including an NEA grant for Poetry, she co-translated *Rilke's Book of Hours* with Joanna Macy. Anita lives and works in Berkeley.

Dan Bellm lives in San Francisco and teaches with California Poets in the Schools. He has published two collections of poetry: *One Hand on the Wheel* and *Buried Treasure*.

Jacqueline Bellon has lived on the San Juan Ridge in Northern California for three decades, where she paints, writes, and gazes at the South Yuba canyon view. She is presently becoming feral.

Thekla Clemens was born, raised, and educated in Germany. She worked as a psychotherapist and traveled extensively overseas in search of spiritual nourishment until landing mysteriously in the foothills of the Sierra, where she lives and writes.

David A. Comstock is an artist, historian, and author of several books, including *Gold Diggers and Camp Followers*, *Brides of the Gold Rush*, and *Greenbacks and Copperheads*.

Gary Cooke is a resident of Grass Valley, California, who has in recent years reactivated his involvement in poetry. The Heyeck Press published his chapbook, *Butterfish and Other Poems*, in 1978.

Judy Brackett Crowe is a Nebraska native who moved to California in 1952. She received a PEN Syndicated Fiction Award for a story broadcast on NPR's "The Sound of Writing." She teaches English and writing at Sierra College and UC Davis Extension.

Doc Dachtler has lived in and about Nevada County for thirty-five years. He worked as a teacher in a one-room school and is presently a carpenter.

Tony D'Arpino has lived in the forests of California, Oregon, and Hawaii. He has had recent work published in *Runes, The Larcom Review*, and *Poetic Matrix*, among others.

Laressa Dickey now writes and paints in Northern California after surviving both a childhood in Tennessee and a BA from the University of Memphis.

Ross Drago was born in Buffalo, New York, and received his BA in Painting and English Literature from Buffalo's S.U.N.Y. in 1964. He moved to Berkeley in 1967 and founded the Energy Art Studio in 1992. Ross is the author of fourteen books of prose.

Charles Entrekin, author of four poetry books, holds an MFA in Creative Writing, founded the Creative Writing Department at John F. Kennedy University and the Berkeley Poets Workshop & Press, and is currently managing editor of Hip Pocket Press.

Demian Entrekin is currently occupied in entrepreneurial endeavors and in raising a two-year-old son with his wife of ten years, Beth. He received his Masters degree from SFSU in English with a focus on critical methodologies.

Gail Rudd Entrekin teaches English and Creative Writing at Sierra College and is Poetry Editor of Hip Pocket Press. Her two books of poetry are *John Danced* (1985) and *You Notice the Body* (1998).

Molly Fisk is the author of four poetry books and is presently at work on a self-help book, *Coming Back to Life: How to Speed Up Your Healing with Poetry.*

Karen Joy Fowler is the author of two story collections and three novels, the third of which, *Sister Noon*, was a finalist for the PEN/ Faulkner award. Her best-known work is the novel *Sarah Canary*, published in 1991.

Molly Giles is the author of a novel, *Iron Shoes*, and two short story collections, *Rough Translations* and *Creek Walk*. She is the Director of the Programs in Creative Writing at the University of Arkansas in Fayetteville.

Oakley Hall is the author of twenty-two novels, including *Warlock*, *The Downhill Racers*, and *The Children of the Sun*, and is founder of the Squaw Valley Community of Writers. He divides his year between San Francisco and Squaw Valley.

Sands Hall is the author of the novel *Catching Heaven* (Ballantine Reader's Circle Selection and Willa Award finalist) and two plays. She teaches and lectures at universities around the nation, and acts, writes, and directs with the Foothill Theatre Company.

Forrest Hamer is the author of two volumes of poetry, *Call & Response* (1995), and *Middle Ear* (2000), winner of the Bay Area Book Reviewers Association Award. He lives and works in the San Francisco East Bay.

Donna Hanelin teaches creative writing in Nevada City and Sacramento, California, and conducts intensive writing retreats in Oaxaca, Mexico. Her first book of poetry, *And I You*, was published by Black Rock Press at the University of Nevada.

Bruce Hawkins sleeps in El Cerrito and hides behind a database in downtown Oakland all day in one of the longest hibernation cycles known to science. He is widely, if infrequently, published.

Jane Hirshfield's fifth poetry collection, *Given Sugar, Given Salt* (HarperCollins, 2001) was a finalist for the National Book Critics Circle Award and winner of the Bay Area Book Reviewers Award. She has received Guggenheim and Rockefeller Foundation fellowships, and her work has appeared in *The Atlantic Monthly*, *The New Yorker*, *The Nation*, and elsewhere.

James D. Houston is the award-winning author of seven novels, most recently *Snow Mountain Passage* (Alfred A. Knopf), cited in *The Washington Post* as "a powerful novel of our shared American destiny." He lives in Santa Cruz.

Jeanne Wakatsuki Houston co-authored the nonfiction classic, *Farewell to Manzanar*, based on her family's experience during the World War II internment. Her novel, *The Legend of Firehorse Woman*, is due in 2003. She lives in Santa Cruz.

Christine Irving began writing professionally during her expatriate years in the Middle East. She is the author of a collection of poetry, *Be a Teller of Tales*, and has been most recently published in ZYZZYVA.

Benjamin Jahn has been a mountain walker since his father took him backpacking in 1983. A graduate of UC Davis in 2000, he is currently at work on a book of stories, one of which has been published in ZYZZYVA. He lives in Berkeley.

Belden Johnson is delighted to be included in this anthology with his son, Nate. When not raising children or writing, Belden works as a psychotherapist at The Primal Center in Nevada City, which he co-founded in 1979 in Berkeley.

Nate Johnson grew up in Nevada City and attended Pomona College. He lives in Barley, Idaho, where he writes for the *Times-News* and acts in a community theater troupe. Nate is currently at work on a collection of stories about his travels in Alaska.

Louis B. Jones is the author of three novels, *Ordinary Money* (Viking/Penguin, 1990), *Particles and Luck* (Vintage/Pantheon, 1994), and *California's Over* (Vintage/Pantheon, 1998). He lives in Nevada City.

Jeff Kane, a medical doctor, is Director of Psychosocial Education at Sierra Nevada Cancer Center in Grass Valley, California. His new book, *The Healing Companion* (HarperSanFrancisco, 2001) is a manual of bedside manner.

George Keithley is the author of eight books of poetry, including the award-winning epic, *The Donner Party*. His writing has appeared in *The New York Times, Harper's* and *TriQuarterly*.

Thomas Kellar, 46, began writing poetry in 1998. He lives with his wife and two sons in the Sierra foothills where he enjoys discordant jazz, cheap cigars, professional basketball, and watching the sunset from the sanctity of a wraparound porch.

Carol Wade Lundberg teaches Creative Writing at Santa Rosa Junior College. Her poetry and short stories have appeared in many literary journals. Her first book of poetry, *The Secret Life*, was published by Mellen Poetry Press.

Ed McClanahan lives in Lexington, Kentucky. His most recent book is *My Vita, If You Will* (Counterpoint, 1998). "Harry at the Breach" is excerpted from his novel-in-progress, *The Return of the Son of Needmore*.

Katherine McCord's poetry manuscript was chosen by Michael Simms as one of four finalists in the Autumn House Press open competition. She teaches Creative Writing/Poetry at New Mexico Institute of Mining and Technology.

Linda Watanabe McFerrin is the author of two poetry collections, a collection of award-winning short stories, *The Hand of Buddha*, and a novel, *Namako: Sea Cucumber*, which was named Best Book for the Teen-Age by the New York Public Library. She won the Katherine Anne Porter Prize for Fiction, and she is an editor of *Best Places Northern California* and publisher of *Wild Writing Women: Stories of World Travel*.

W. Scott McLean and his wife Patricia are founding members of the Ring of Bone Zendo in Nevada City, California. He earned a Ph.D. in German Literature from UC Santa Barbara and teaches in the programs in Nature & Culture and Comparative Literature at UC Davis. In 1980 he edited Gary Snyder's *The Real Work* for New Directions.

Alicia Suskin Ostriker is the author of ten volumes of poetry, including *The Crack in Everything* (1996) and *The Little Space: Poems Selected and New, 1968-1998* (1998), both finalists for the National Book Award, and *The Imaginary Lover* (1986), winner of the William Carlos Williams Award.

Utah Phillips is an engaging rogue prone to a certain Japhetic dromomania. He is one of America's most feared folksingers. "Mors ante servitium!"

Carlos Reyes' most recent book of poetry is *A Suitcase Full of Crows* (1995). His latest book of translations is *Poemas de la Isla/Island Poems* by Josefina de la Torre (Eastern Washington University, 2000).

Marilee Richards' latest book of poetry is *A Common Ancestor* (Hip Pocket Press, 1998). She lives in Sedona, Arizona.

Sandra Rockman is a writer, playwright, and theater director who has lived and worked in the Sierra foothills since 1978. She is currently at work on a novel.

Steve Sanfield has more than two dozen books of poetry, folklore, mythology, and children's tales to his credit. He has been honored by the American Library Association, the International Reading Association, the Bay Area Book Reviewer's Association, and the haiku journal, *HaikuSashiZo*. He lives on the San Juan Ridge of Northern California, where he founded and organized the recently concluded Sierra Storytelling Festival.

Gary Short's second book of poems, *Flying Over Sonny Liston*, received the Western States Book Award. He has been a Stegner Fellow at Stanford University and a resident of the Fine Arts Work Center in Provincetown, as well as a professor at several other universities. He currently divides his time between Virginia City, Nevada, and Guatemala.

Claudette Mork Sigg won the Steelhead Literary Contest for poetry in 1996, and her work was published in *Translations from the Human Language, A Poetry Audio Tour of Selected Works from the Oakland Museum of California's Gallery of California Art.*

Gary Snyder, one of the original "beats," is America's foremost environmental poet. He was born in San Francisco and has spent most of his life in Northern California. He is the author of 17 books of poetry, essays and interviews including *Turtle Island*, which won the Pulitzer Prize for Poetry in 1974, and most recently the inclusive edition of *Mountains and Rivers Without End* in 1996.

Kathryn Napier Stull is assistant editor of Hip Pocket Press, is pursuing a degree in creative writing, and studies poetry with Gail Entrekin.

Daniel Williams has lived in the Sierra for thirty years and seeks in his poems to forge a link between contemporary humanity and the wondrous primal spirit of this bio-region. A longstanding member of *Poets and Writers*, he makes his residence in Yosemite.

Steve Wilson was featured in *American Poetry: The Next Generation* (Carnegie-Mellon) and has new work appearing in *Commonweal*, *Flyway*, *New Orleans Review*, and *Midwest Quarterly*. His books include *Allegory Dance* and *The Singapore Express*.

Gregg Wiltshire has been a student, teacher, practicing father, lousy son, bartender, barfly, husband, and peddler of food, wine, books, pictures, things that matter and things that don't. Currently he is more or less happy with his lot.

Susan Goldsmith Wooldridge is author of *poemcrazy: freeing your life with words* (Three Rivers/Random House), now in its 16th printing. She is currently at work on a new book on collage and writing. Susan lives in Chico, California.

Printed in the United States
762400002B

9 780917 658327